FROM
LEE
TO
LI

Also by Ben Stevens
A Gaijin's Guide to Japan

FROM
LEE
TO
LI

An A – Z Guide of
Martial Arts Heroes

Ben Stevens

FRIDAY
BOOKS

The Friday Project
An imprint of HarperCollins Publishers
77–85 Fulham Palace Road
Hammersmith, London W6 8JB
www.thefridayproject.co.uk
www.harpercollins.co.uk

First published by The Friday Project in 2009

A catalogue record for this book
is available from the British Library

ISBN 978-1-906321-86-4

Designed and typeset by Maggie Dana
Illustrations by Jorge Santillan

Printed and bound in Great Britain by
Clays Ltd, St Ives plc

Mixed Sources
Product group from well-managed
forests and other controlled sources
www.fsc.org Cert no. SW-COC-1806
© 1996 Forest Stewardship Council
FSC

FSC is a non-profit international organisation established to promote
the responsible management of the world's forests. Products carrying
the FSC label are independently certified to assure consumers that
they come from forests that are managed to meet the social, eco-
nomic and ecological needs of present or future generations.

Find out more about HarperCollins and the environment at
www.harpercollins.co.uk/green

Dedicated to the memory of Nakamura Sensei,
my instructor and friend

INTRODUCTION

Few subjects are as prone to myth, exaggeration and general controversy as the martial arts. In *From Lee to Li*, however, I have set out to record, as accurately as is possible, some of those many men and women who have, throughout history, 'served' the martial arts in a way that is out of the ordinary.

Some (**Jigoro Kano, Chang San-Feng**) evolved a new style. Others developed an existing form, or established a career – for example, in the film industry (**Jackie Chan, Jean-Claude Van Damme**) – through their martial skills. Then there are those who, like **Bruce Lee** and **Carlos Gracie**, caused what was nothing short of a martial arts' revolution.

From China to Croatia, Brazil to Great Britain – and from before the birth of Christ right up to the present day – *From Lee to Li* contains well over 100 accounts of those who have helped shape the fascinating world of martial arts.

Ben Stevens began practising judō aged seven, and since then has studied various martial arts but particularly judō, jujutsu and karate. He would like to extend special thanks to Salah Alkawari for his detailed comments and advice concerning this book.

A

ADAMS, NEIL

Born in 1958, and having started *judō* aged seven, Neil Adams MBE has the distinction of being Britain's first male World Judō Champion (receiving a gold medal in 1981), as well as receiving silver medals at the 1980 and 1984 Olympic Games. His autobiography, *A Life in Judo*, demonstrates his fiery will to win, and hatred of losing.

Initially known for his powerful throws – particularly *tai-otoshi* or 'body drop' – his defeat to a French opponent, when aged twenty, made him focus intensively on *newaza*, or grappling. Soon, his *newaza* techniques were recognised as being some of the finest in professional *judō* – and it was his trademark arm locks in particular that were feared by those who had to face him. (According to journalist and *judō* practitioner,

Mark Law, in his definitive book *The Pyjama Game: A Journey into Judo*, any opponent of Adam's who found himself grappling with him, would '... soon hear their coaches at the matside screaming warnings at them to get on their feet'.) Adams kept detailed logs concerning both his own and his opponents' performances, and was pushed to the very limits of physical endurance by such trainers as **Brian Jacks**.

For a time the darling of the British media (due partly to his on-off relationship with Olympic swimmer Sharron Davies), Neil Adams now runs a Corporate Health Programme with his Canadian-born wife, Niki, who is herself a *judō* Olympian. (The pair met while they were both commentating at the 2 000 Sydney Olympic Games.) At the time of writing, Adams is a seventh *dan judoka* (*judō* practitioner).

AKIYAMA, YOSHITOKI SHIROBEI

During the seventeenth century (although some sources put the date at up to 200 years earlier), Akiyama, a Japanese physician born in Nagasaki, travelled to China in order to improve his medical knowledge. Whilst in China, however, he also studied an ancient martial art known variously as either *Hakuda* or *Baida*. *Hakuda* or *Baida* showed a practitioner the most lethal parts of the human body to strike – but also taught how it was possible to resuscitate someone from the brink of death.

Returning to Japan armed with this new knowledge, Akiyama opened his own martial arts' school; but his methods were generally considered to be crude and limited, and those students who joined soon left. Greatly disillusioned, Akiyama retreated to a remote shrine for 100 days to think and meditate.

Towards the end of this period of isolation, Akiyama was profoundly affected by the sight of a pine tree that – rigid and unyielding as it was – was severely damaged during a snow storm. The snow accumulated upon the branches until the sheer weight of it caused the limbs to snap. However, a nearby willow tree yielded and bent, thereby surviving the storm completely unscathed.

This caused Akiyama to evolve a large number of what he called 'natural movements', and again start another martial arts' school – this time with far greater success. He named his style *yoshin-ryu*, or 'willow heart school'.

B

BARTON-WRIGHT, EDWARD WILLIAM

Long before **Jon Bluming**, Donald 'Donn' Frederick Draeger and **Robert W. Smith** – all martial artists who helped to introduce Asian fighting styles to the West – there was the Englishman Edward William Barton-Wright.

Born in 1860, Barton-Wright (a civil engineer by trade) went to Japan when aged thirty-three, where he stayed for four years. There he trained in a number of different *jujitsu* (there are various spellings) styles in Kobe, Yokohama, and Tokyo, and was so impressed by what he learned that he made the rather confident claim that '... (any) man who attacks you with a knife or other weapon can be easily disarmed'.

But even before his trip to Japan, Barton-Wright was

an expert in several Western fighting styles, including boxing, fencing, wrestling, and *savate*. In order to test the practical application of such arts, he was apparently in the habit of 'engaging toughs' (i.e. picking fights) in various seedy places, such as inns and music halls.

Upon his return to England, Barton-Wright found that many questioned whether this strange martial art he'd brought back with him was actually any good. The simplest way to prove that it *was*, decided Barton-Wright, was to challenge his doubters to a fight. Though even then he couldn't really win: soundly thrashing a wrestling champion called Mr Chipchase, he was subsequently accused of cheating – the mysterious throws, locks and holds of *jujitsu* being classed as 'unsporting'. (Mr Chipchase himself, however, was gracious in defeat, and positively gushing about *jujitsu* declared that its '... system of defence and retaliation is so much more scientific than my own style'.)

Barton-Wright went on to found his own *dōjō* (Japanese for 'training hall') within England, where he mixed *jujitsu* with the other fighting arts he also knew – such as boxing and fencing – resulting in his own, unique style that he labelled 'Bartitsu'. (So popular did Bartitsu prove – if only fleetingly – that it was mentioned in the 1903 Sherlock Holmes' short story *The Adventure of the Empty House*. In this, the resurrected Holmes informs Doctor Watson that his victory over his arch-nemesis Professor Moriarty at the Reichenbach Falls was due to his '... knowledge of *baritsu* [*sic*], or the Japanese system of wrestling'. Note here the accidental misspelling of Barton-Wright's style.)

Unfortunately, Bartitsu's popularity had quite declined by around 1920; and by the time Barton-Wright died in 1951, aged ninety, he was all but a pauper. However, he can certainly be remembered as being one of the true pioneers of 'mixed' or 'hybrid' martial arts – having demonstrated the idea that techniques from various different styles can, and should, be put together to form the most efficient way of fighting.

BENKEI, SAITO MUSASHIBO

A much-loved folk hero of Japan, Saito Musashibo Benkei was either: a) the supernatural offspring of a temple god, or b) the son of a blacksmith's daughter, depending on which story you choose to believe. (Personally, I tend to go with the latter.)

Apparently coming into the world with hair and teeth already in place, Benkei was a natural troublemaker – so much so that he soon earned the nickname *oniwaka* or 'young devil child'.

In spite of this, he trained as a monk and, at the age of seventeen, stood two metres tall with the strength of a small bull. It was at this point that he decided he'd had enough of living in a Buddhist temple. What he *really* wanted to do, he decided, was to join the *yam-*

abushi – a sect of mountain priests who were also quite adept at fighting.

So, now trained in martial arts and warfare (and particularly expert in his use of the sword), Benkei decided to place himself by Gojo Bridge in Kyoto, where he set himself a target of beating 1000 men using his sword.

He almost succeeded; 999 men proved absolutely no problem whatsoever, but it was the very last man who was to be Benkei's undoing. Along he came, playing a tune on his flute, a little sword hanging by his side.

'He looks easy enough,' Benkei said gleefully to himself. 'Certainly easier than some of the other men I've had to fight.'

As the man grew closer, Benkei called, 'Hey, you. Just hand over that sword, eh? That is, if you want to continue breathing!'

'You idiot,' scoffed the slightly-built man. 'I am Minamoto no Yoshitsune, son of the infamous warlord Minamoto no Yoshitomo. Step aside this instant, or taste my wrath!'

'You're for it,' growled Benkei as he rushed forwards.

Yoshitsune, however, merely stepped aside before using his flute to hit the giant sharply around the head. Benkei let out a roar and flashed his great sword all around him, but each time Yoshitsune was simply not there.

So undemanding did Yoshitsune find the battle that

he was frequently able to play a tune on his flute in the course of it. Finally, exhausted with cutting through nothing but thin air, Benkei sat on the ground and conceded defeat.

'Okay, you win,' he told Yoshitsune. 'Here, take my sword, as proof that you're the better man.'

But Yoshitsune only laughed as he sat down beside the dejected giant. He explained that he'd been trained in martial arts and swordsmanship by supernatural goblins called *tengu*, and so only needed to draw his sword in moments of extreme peril.

'I'm sorry, Benkei,' said Yoshitsune gently, 'but this was a battle I knew I'd win before you even challenged me.'

It was at this point that Benkei begged to become Yoshitsune's loyal follower, for however long they both should live.

So from that day on they had a multitude of adventures, until the day finally came when Yoshitsune found himself betrayed by his powerful brother, Minamoto Yoritomo. Holed up in Takadachi Castle, an entire army just about to force their way inside, Yoshitsune killed first his family and then himself, to prevent them from falling into enemy hands.

Benkei, loyal to the last, remained outside the room where his fallen master lay, defending it until his great body was finally brought down by over 100 arrows.

BIMBA, MESTRE

Born Manuel dos Reis Machado, *Mestre* referred to the fact that Machado was a 'master' of Capoeira, a martial art created by enslaved Africans in Brazil during the fifteenth and sixteenth centuries.

Bimba, meanwhile, was the slang for 'penis' – apparently at his birth there was some confusion over Machado's gender, until a midwife thought to take notice of the baby's male part.

At its conception, Capoeira served a number of uses: it was a way for the slaves to stay healthy and to learn self-defence skills, while to those onlookers watching the 'fights' it acted as entertainment and a general way of raising the spirits.

I use quotation marks for the word fights as Capoeira's fundamental purpose – that of teaching self-defence – was heavily disguised. Due to the techniques used it could look as much like a dance as a fight, and was anyway often accompanied by music, chanting, and singing. Thus anyone watching who might otherwise have been concerned by the fact that the slaves were learning to fight (for example, the slaves' owner) would be lulled into thinking that the slaves were merely amusing themselves with a bit of singing and dancing. (Something that was doubtless deemed acceptable by a more 'liberal' slave-owner.)

Following the abolition of slavery in 1888, Capoeira ironically had to be practised in even greater secrecy as it was associated with the violent street gangs of Brazil. If caught, its practitioners were punished severely – some having the tendons of their feet cut by the police.

Finally, however, legal persecution of the martial art ceased and in 1932 Mestre Bimba (then aged thirty-two) was able to open the first Capoeira 'school'. Members were obliged to wear a clean white uniform and conduct themselves well both inside and out of the training hall, and because of this professional people, such as doctors and lawyers, felt that they could now take up Capoeira. So, at last, Capoeira became acceptable to society as a whole.

BLUMING, JON

Jon Bluming was born on 3 February, 1933 in Amsterdam, Holland. Growing up in a Jewish neighbourhood, he witnessed numerous atrocities conducted by the German SS during the Second World War. In fact, Bluming's father was for a time forced into slave labour by the occupying forces, something that obliged Bluming to fend for himself, his mother, and his grandparents while still a child.

Bluming applied to enter the Dutch marines when aged sixteen and was sent to bootcamp. Then, in 1950, the Korean War broke out and Bluming saw action. He was soon wounded with two shots to his upper right leg and sent to a hospital in Tokyo.

During his convalescence he slipped out to the legendary Kodokan (*judō* headquarters), where he saw a breathtaking martial arts' display by a wizened old man who was throwing around much larger men 'like rag dolls'. Bluming suspected then that *judō* – and martial arts in general – was the way to go for a strapping young man with iron in his soul.

He returned to action long enough to get wounded again (this time by a hand grenade) and while recuperating – on this occasion in a Korean hospital – Bluming studied *tae kwon do* for six weeks under a teacher called Yong Dong Po.

Bluming returned to Holland but soon decided that civvie life was not for him; within a matter of months he was back in Korea. Then, during a particularly fierce night of fighting, he was wounded yet again by a mortar. At that point, even Bluming decided that enough was enough and so he returned to Holland.

When he arrived in Amsterdam he saw a poster for a local *judō* club, the 'Tung Jen', where within twelve months he'd achieved his first *dan* black belt, as well as becoming captain of the club's team.

Disaster struck as he was going for his third *dan*, with Bluming breaking his big toe. It seemed as though he'd have to be content with being second *dan* for a while longer – until Bluming decided to settle the matter by winding the offending toe around and around. He wet himself and nearly passed out with the pain, but upon completing his ad hoc surgery, found that his toe no longer bothered him.

He went on to obtain the desired *dan* grade, in the process performing recognised throws upon seventy-five *judoka* (*judō* practitioners) within twenty-six minutes. Any celebrations were marred soon after when Bluming broke his right knee, requiring an operation and yet another spell in hospital.

It was Bluming's dream to get back to Japan – that magical land he'd had a brief glimpse of while resident at a Tokyo hospital – but for the time being he had to content himself with teaching *judō* first in Germany (at a Berlin police club) and then in Canada, earning the princely sum of two dollars an hour.

In 1959, Bluming left Canada to hitch a ride with some truck-driver friends across the USA, stopping at any number of *dōjō* en-route to train and challenge anyone who fancied their chances. Predictably, Bluming emerged from every altercation the victor.

Bluming did finally get back to Japan, where he quickly earned himself the nickname *Oranda no Dobutsu* (the 'Dutch Animal') for his ferocious style of fighting. He was admired and detested in equal measure by Japanese martial artists, especially when he succeeded in choking one of their number out cold with a strangle.

Such tales concerning Bluming's infamy in Japan spread far and wide, prompting an offer that he return to Holland and teach. The contract was too good to turn down, and so Bluming at last left Japan for his country of birth.

Later, Bluming's *sensei* (Japanese for 'teacher' – approximately translates as 'one who has gone before') in Japan – the legendary **Masutatsu 'Mas' Oyama** – awarded Bluming (Oyama's first foreign student) a sixth *dan* in *karate*, with many oriental martial artists demanding to know how a foreigner could be ranked so highly. Oyama replied that anyone was freely entitled to address such a question to Bluming personally: if they managed to beat him in a fight, then he (Oyama) would pay them $100 000 and strip Bluming of his ranking.

Only one man took Oyama up on his offer – a Korean *tae kwon do* expert called Kwan Mo Gun. Gun was first knocked out by two of Bluming's students, who explained their actions thus: 'If you go first, Sensei, there'll be nothing left after.'

But each time Gun was knocked out he quickly awoke and got back up, saying 'And now Bluming ...' Bluming had to admire the man's guts, even as he beat him.

An even higher grade – in fact the very highest grade it is possible to attain – was given to Bluming upon the death of Mas Oyama in 1994. Bluming was now a tenth *dan karateka* (he has also a ninth *dan* in *judō*), and acknowledged worldwide as the real deal when it came to martial arts and self-defence.

He continues to travel the world teaching and lecturing, never afraid to publicly rubbish anyone he suspects of being a fraud or a fake in the martial arts' world. (For an example of this, just check out the 'Expelled Members' section of his website.)

He also dismisses certain elements of *karate kata* (a serious of pre-set movements) as being a way for poor-quality *sensei* to use up the hours they should rather spend teaching their students how to fight.

Apart from warfare, Bluming has had numerous violent encounters on the street. One of which – between Bluming and five pimps, one of whom hit him with a hammer – ended badly for the aggressor. Bluming hit the pimp back and the man subsequently died in hospital. (Since then – unless his life absolutely depends on it – Bluming has vowed never again to hit anyone with a closed fist.)

Such encounters give the reason for Bluming's martial arts' philosophy: if it works, use it – never mind what style it's from – and if it doesn't (like various types of *kata*), forget it.

BODHIDHARMA

Legends concerning Bodhidharma abound, which makes discerning any real facts about him something of an impossible task. For example, he liked to walk everywhere, but was on occasion apparently able to float across a river on a large leaf.

What we *can* say with a reasonable degree of certainty is that he was a wandering Buddhist monk who lived sometime around the sixth century, and that he came to China from India.

It's been suggested that Bodhidharma was from a young age an expert at *kalaripayattu* (often translated as 'practising the arts of the battlefield'), a 3000-year-old martial art that originated in South India, and is to this day practised to promote fluid, animal-like movements and a distinct feeling of inner peace.

Coming to China, Bodhidharma encountered a group of monks who'd grown fat and sluggish, too used to prayer and a lack of physical exercise. To counter this, Bodhidharma taught them what the Japanese refer to as *kata* in the martial arts (a series of pre-set movements), at which the monks became expert, thus establishing the martial arts in China.

Or (according to a different legend) he entered a period of deep meditation, sitting facing a wall within the Shaolin ('young forest') Temple for *nine years*. When he finally got back up and left, he left behind him an iron chest full of manuscripts detailing the secrets of the martial arts, which the monks diligently studied following his departure.

Supporters of the belief that the martial arts originated in India and from there spread out East, like to relay the above stories. While others – who believe that man's ability and willingness to fight is, and never has been, particular to any one country – prefer to keep a more open mind.

BRIGGS, KAREN 'THE WHIPPET'

Forty-five at the time of writing, Karen Briggs has been World Judō Champion no less than four times. (She first won the title in 1982, aged eighteen, and success-fully defended it at the 1984, 1986 and 1989 Judō World Championships.) She was twelve years old when she began practising *judō,* having previously been obsessed with becoming a professional footballer.

Known as 'The Whippet', Briggs would commonly 'warm up' for an intensive *judō* training session with a 6- to 8-mile run. The only thing that ever slowed her down were injuries – these included a broken leg (sus-tained while attempting to throw an opponent), and a right shoulder which was prone to popping out of its socket. Indeed, it was this troublesome shoulder that was responsible for finally ending Brigg's career; in the 1992 Barcelona Olympics, Brigg's much younger oppo-nent – the Japanese female *judoka* Ryoko Tamura (who had, ironically, previously declared that she idolised Briggs) – deliberately targeted the damaged part, something which enabled her to secure victory.

Karen Briggs now runs a *judō* club for children in her native Hull, East Yorkshire. In August 2008, she revealed that she'd recently had a breast removed due to cancer, but with typical fighting spirit went on to state that the '... future looks good'.

BROWN, DENNIS

One of the first Americans (or so it's claimed) to train in the martial arts in mainland China, Dennis Brown gave up a promising career as a computer technician at the age of twenty so he could concentrate fully on being a *kung-fu* instructor.

Following his training in China, he was able to open his own school in the United States, and soon grew so well-known that he was called upon to act in the martial arts' movies that were being made in Hong Kong and Taiwan.

The Chinese Embassy in Washington DC has made Brown their 'Official Consultant of Wushu for the People's Republic of China' (*wushu* is Chinese for 'martial arts'), and in 2000 the magazine *Black Belt* listed him as being one of the '25 Most Influential Martial Artists of the Twentieth Century'.

Brown, meanwhile, continues to emphasise the fact that the martial arts should be a way for people to improve their characters – not just learn how to fight.

BUDDHABHADRA

More simply known as 'Batuo', Buddhabhadra was a wandering Buddhist monk from India who has been immortalised as the founder of the Shaolin Temple, which is synonymous with *wushu* in China.

Batuo drifted into China around 464 AD, where he began preaching Buddhism. It must have taken him a while to achieve the necessary popularity, because only in 495 AD did the Emperor Xiaowendi (at the time busy with his attempts to make Northern China more united, including forcing its inhabitants to wear the traditional garb) give permission and the necessary funds for a *shaolin si* ('young forest temple') to be built as Batuo's base.

It was, by all accounts, something of a modest structure, with a round dome as its shrine and a small platform where Indian and Chinese monks translated Buddhist texts from Indian into Chinese.

It's worth noting here that, at that time in China, Buddhism was praised more as being an educational system concerning how one should lead one's life, rather than as a religion.

Thus, under Xiaowendi's rule life did get a bit easier for his subjects. Short periods of imprisonment replaced mutilation as a punishment for many (not particularly serious) crimes, while the sick and the poor could expect to receive a certain amount of what we might now refer to as 'care in the community'.

C

CASSEUX, MICHEL

Michel Casseux (1794–1869) was a pharmacist who did much to develop the French martial art of *savate* (pronounced '*sa-vat*'), also known as *boxe Française,* or 'French boxing.'

Evolving out of Parisian street fighting techniques that were, for whatever reason, particularly popular with sailors – including high kicks and 'slaps' rather than punches (to avoid the legal penalty for using a closed fist) – *savate* (the French for 'old shoe' or 'old boot' – presumably a useful piece of footwear to wear during combat) was given a number of rules by Casseux, such as no headbutting, biting, or eye gouging.

A *savate* practitioner (if male, known as a *savateur*; *savateuse,* if female) was at something of an advantage when facing a boxer, as *savate* made – and continues to make – free use of such 'standard' martial arts' leg techniques as a roundhouse kick. (Only the feet may be used when kicking; knees and shins are strictly forbidden.)

CHAN, HEUNG

The founder of the *kung-fu* system named *Choy Lee Fut*, Chan Heung was born in 1806. From an early age he was an avid student of *kung-fu* (first taught by his uncle, a *Shaolin* fighting monk), then in his early twenties he sought to expand his knowledge by seeking out a hermit named Choy Fook. (Choy, a former monk and martial arts' legend in his own lifetime, lived on a nearby mountain. He apparently had a number of ugly scars on his head, which had resulted in his unfortunate nickname 'Rotten Head Fook'.)

After some months of searching, Chan Heung eventually succeeded in finding Choy Fook, who seems not to have been particularly fond of company. Chan then trained under Choy for around a decade, eventually pioneering his own system which he named after Choy Fook and another teacher who'd instructed him, Lee Yau-Shan. (The *Fut* in the title, incidentally, is Cantonese for 'Buddha' – something which Chan Heung believed imparted a 'spiritual' element to the system he'd evolved.)

Having fought against the British in China's Opium Wars, Chan Heung later went to San Francisco, where he opened his own *kwoon* (martial arts' training hall). He died in 1875.

CHAN, JACKIE

Born in Hong Kong on 7 April, 1954, Jackie's parents christened him Chan Kong-sang, meaning 'born in Hong Kong'. (Just in case there should have been any confusion over the matter, presumably.)

Almost as soon as he could walk, Chan was practising *kung-fu* with his father each morning, which it was hoped would help to instill such noble attributes as honesty, courage, and perseverance into the young boy.

When Chan was seven years old, his father was offered a job as a cook in the American Embassy in Australia. So off he and his wife went, leaving young Jackie in the tender loving care of the Peking Opera School.

Actually, there was nothing very tender or loving about the school. The child students there were drilled relentlessly in the martial arts, singing, acting, and acrobatics – all skills they would need for their intended life with the Peking Opera. The children were expected to learn quickly – and learn quickly they did; that is, if they wished to avoid being beaten and otherwise reprimanded in no uncertain terms.

Chan made his acting debut, aged eight, in the snap-
pily entitled *Seven Little Valiant Fighters: Big and
Little Wong Tin Bar,* and as he got a little older, found
work as an extra in various other, long-forgotten films.
He graduated from the Academy aged seventeen, only
to discover that the Peking Opera would now not be
requiring his services after all – it was no longer very
popular, and was thus in the middle of firing rather
than hiring.

Further limiting Chan's employment opportunities
was the fact that he could neither read nor write – two
skills the Academy had apparently neglected to teach
their students as they jumped through suspended hoops
while singing operatic airs.

Desperate, Chan decided to become a stuntman,
quickly earning a reputation for his almost suicidal
lack of fear. Even seasoned professionals shied away
from some of the stunts Chan was prepared to enter-
tain, although to Chan it all came down to one simple
choice: do the job and eat, or walk away and starve.

For a while he was doing reasonably well (he made a
blink-and-you'll-miss-it appearance in **Bruce Lee's**
Enter the Dragon), until the Hong Kong film industry
started to do badly, and then even Chan had trouble
finding work.

Running out of money, Chan was obliged to move to
Australia to be with his parents. By all accounts he
hated his time there, doing nothing more than menial

construction jobs, although something came out of it that boded well for the future. One of Chan's co-workers, who was having trouble pronouncing his full name, took to calling him just 'Jackie' instead

Then, pretty much out of the blue, Chan was contacted by one Willie Chan, who was working within the newly revitalised Hong Kong film industry.

'I've been watching some of your stunts, and every one's fantastic,' said Willie. 'How would you like to come back to Hong Kong and star in a film called *New Fist of Fury*?'

'I'm on the plane already,' replied the 21-year-old Jackie, tired and filthy after yet another day spent working as a casual labourer.

New Fist of Fury was followed by a number of other films starring Chan, but it was only when he began to put his own ideas into the plots that he became a genuine star; producing such gems as *Drunken Master* in 1978.

Popular as he may have been in Asia – and Hong Kong in particular (where his nickname continues to be 'Big Brother') – success in the West would elude Chan for a long time. Only with 1996's *Rumble in the Bronx* did Chan become a notable box-office success, capitalising on this with later films such as *Rush Hour* and *Shanghai Noon*.

It's well known that Chan has broken umpteen bones, including his neck, while performing his own stunts; and he even came close to death on one occasion when he fractured his skull while filming 1987's *Armour of God*. As a result of this he suffers from chronic pain, and these days relies – though not always – upon stunt doubles, as it would otherwise be next to impossible to find an insurance company prepared to underwrite his productions.

He has in recent years sought to diversify from roles which feature his martial arts' prowess (as well as his standard, 'slightly-goofy-but-basically-a-nice-guy' character), resulting in films including *The Myth* – in which he played both a general in ancient China as well as a modern-day archaeologist – and *Rob-B-Hood*, in which Chan played a 'comical' criminal who kidnaps a baby.

Since the mid-1980s, Chan has forged a separate career as a pop star, singing in a variety of languages (including English and Japanese) and releasing over 20 albums. He also works tirelessly for a number of charities, including those that deal with environmental issues and animal rights, and has paid for several schools to be built in the poorer areas of China.

CHANG, SAN-FENG

The semi-mythical 'founder' (this is still hotly contested by many) of what is known in the West as *tai chi chuan*, or the 'supreme ultimate fist'.

Establishing any concrete facts about Mr Chang San-Feng is nigh-on impossible. For example, the date

of his birth is variously estimated to have been between 600 AD and the sixteenth century. Rumours also abound that he achieved immortality (though where he is now is anyone's guess), was over seven foot tall, could cover more than 300 miles in a single day (on foot), and that for whatever reason he wore on his head a large cymbal instead of a hat, which only the 'privileged' (whoever they might have been) were permitted to sound.

However, Chang San-Feng may have been a *Shaolin* monk, active sometime towards the end of the twelfth century, who for over a decade engaged in strenuous *kung-fu* training. But whilst out walking one day, he was captivated by a fight between a snake and a bird.

The bird was larger and seemed more powerful – there was little doubt that it would be able to kill and devour the snake – and yet, by suddenly feigning weakness, the snake caused the bird to become overconfident. Carelessly it soared down upon its seemingly stricken prey, only to be grabbed in the snake's jaws and killed.

Chang San-Feng was dumbfounded. Here, provided by nature itself, was the answer to all the questions and doubts he'd privately had concerning his martial arts' training.

Shrewdly, he copied the snake's example of cunning and speed over superior strength, combining this with his own ideas concerning 'chi' or a person's own inner power (for example, what sometimes – incredibly –

allows a mother to lift a burning car to free her trapped child) and adding a more 'spiritual' dimension to the martial arts than had existed previously.

CHENG, MAN-CH'ING

Born in 1902, Cheng Man-ch'ing achieved the modest title 'The Master of Five Excellences' due to his expertise in poetry, medicine, painting, calligraphy, and last, but most definitely not least, *tai ji quan* (more popularly known in the West as *tai chi chuan*). Cheng was fond of referring to himself as 'the old child who never tires of learning', and in his later years could be heard bemoaning the fact that old age had caught him unawares.

He was nine years old when he was struck on the head by a rock or a brick, which for a short while placed him in a coma and erased his memory. To aid his recuperation, he was apprenticed to a well-known painter, who soon discovered that the young boy was no slouch with a brush himself. In time, Cheng was able to provide for his family by selling his own paintings.

In his late twenties he began a serious study of *tai ji quan* as a way of counteracting tuberculosis, which he'd contracted a short while earlier. (Given that he lived until he was seventy-three, we can assume that his novel approach to a cure was successful.) The style of *tai chi* which he evolved is still widely practised today.

CHEUNG, KU YU

Old, black-and-white photographs abound of Grand-master Ku Yu Cheung bending a steel bar around his arm, having a large boulder placed on his stomach, being smashed over the head with a lump of quarry stone, breaking twelve bricks with the palm of his hand, and so on.

Certainly, early on in his life, nothing indicated that Cheung would one day be capable of performing such feats. This was in spite of the fact that his father was a famous martial artist, who acted as an 'escort' to wealthy merchants who would otherwise be plagued by robbers and other assorted ne'er-do-wells as they travelled throughout China on business. So successful was Cheung's father that he established a business employing some 200 martial arts' experts, all acting as escorts or bodyguards for those who could afford their services. Through this, Cheung's father could afford to send his quiet, bookish son to an exclusive private school.

Only on his deathbed did his father apparently plead with Ku Yu to train in the martial arts, and so off went the teenager to a *kung-fu* master named Yim Kai Wun.

In the ensuing eleven years, Cheung learned – amongst many other things – leg techniques, breath control and *Gum Jung Chi Gung* or 'iron shirt' – the art of making the body withstand any blow.

The news that his mother had passed away caused

Cheung to finally leave his *sifu,* or 'teacher', and return home. As he did so, Yim Kai Wun gave his departing student one last piece of advice:

'Through your *kung-fu* training you have succeeded in climbing one mountain, but just remember – there is always another.'

Later, sometime around the mid-1920s, Cheung was appointed bodyguard to the Secretary of Finance, and then became Chief Instructor in the Martial Arts to the military. One of his 'party tricks' was to have a car filled with three students driven over his shirtless body.

A story concerning Cheung details how he accepted a bet that he wouldn't be able to withstand a kick from a horse. Proving that he in fact could, he then insisted that he be allowed to hit the horse back – something which caused the unfortunate creature to expire soon after. (Outwardly, the horse bore hardly any trace of having received a blow. When an 'autopsy' – of sorts – was performed, however, it was discovered that most of its internal organs had been ruptured. Such was the lethal power of Cheung's 'iron hand'.)

CHIN, GEN PINH

A Buddhist monk who came to Japan from China around 1559, bringing with him his knowledge of what the Japanese referred to as *kempo* or *kenpo* – the 'law of the fist'. Following Chin Gen Pinh's demonstrations of what he knew, parts of kempo were quickly assimilated into the type of *jujitsu* being taught to samurai warriors at that time.

CHIN, LIP MON

An 'iron palm' practitioner (*See* **Sing Pak,** for more information about iron palm) and drunkard who, after a night of wine-fuelled debauchery, found himself fighting empty-handed against a tiger. Due to his mastery of iron palm, however, Chin Lip Mon was able to kill the creature.

The following morning, none of the villagers living nearby believed Chin Lip Mon when he told them what had happened.

'Bah! You're making it up,' they scoffed, until Chin Lip Mon led them into a forest where the deceased tiger lay.

'We take it back,' said the villagers in awed tones. 'And from now on, we're going to call you "Tiger Master".'

This victory caused Chin Lip Mon to get his act together, stop drinking (as much), and open up a *kung-fu* school.

CHOI, HONG HI

The purported founder of *tae kwon do* (although this is contested by some), Choi was born in 1918 in the remote Hwa Dae, Myong Chun district of what is now

North Korea. He was a somewhat frail and sickly child (this seems to be something of a pattern for famous 'founding fathers' of martial arts – refer here to **Morihei Ueshiba**).

Aged twelve, Choi was expelled from school for protesting against the Japanese authorities who were then in control of Korea. His father sent him to learn calligraphy – although so alarmed was the new teacher by Choi's lamentable physical condition that he also arranged to have him taught the martial art of *taek kyeon* ('foot techniques') as well.

Choi went to Japan in 1937, where within two years he'd become a black belt in *karate*. With the outbreak of the Second World War, Choi was forced to enlist in the Japanese army. However, when his links with the Korean Independence Movement were uncovered he was arrested, tried, and thrown into a cell.

This gave Choi some much-needed time and solitude in which to practise the martial art that would become *tae kwon do*. Soon the other prisoners were demanding that Choi teach them a little of what he knew – and Choi readily obliged. Finally, the situation threatened to descend into farce as even the jailers requested that their prisoner teach them what was – at heart – a mixture of *taek kyeon* and *karate*.

Choi was freed in August 1945 (according to some sources, just days before he was due to be executed for 'treason'), and made his way to Seoul. There he was soon promoted to the rank of Lieutenant (ultimately he'd become a Major-General) in the South Korean army, taking this opportunity to teach soldiers – both American as well as Korean – *tae kwon do*.

In 1955, *tae kwon do* ('the way of the feet and the hands') was formally recognised within Korea, with a special administrative board being appointed, and from there word concerning this new martial art soon spread across the globe. It became an official Olympic sport for the first time at the 2000 Summer Olympics in Sydney. (The middleweight gold medal that year was won by Cuban Ángel Matos, who was, however, disqualified for life in 2008 after he intentionally kicked a referee in the face at the Beijing Olympics.)

CHOI, YONG SUL

The founder of the Korean martial art of *hapkido*, Choi (born in 1904) always claimed to have been abducted, aged eight, from his village in present-day South Korea by – of all people – a Japanese confectionary maker. (There exist, however, several conflicting stories concerning Choi's early years.)

The man abandoned the child in Moji, Japan, and Choi made his way to Osaka, where he was picked up by the police and placed in a Buddhist temple in Kyoto that cared for orphans.

In the two or so years that he spent at this temple-cum-orphanage, Choi had a particularly miserable time. Endlessly bullied because of his nationality and the fact that he couldn't speak Japanese very well, he reacted in the only way he was able – with his fists.

Finally, the temple abbot thought to ask Choi where he saw his life going, and the young Korean replied that he was extremely interested in learning a martial art.

By a stroke of good fortune (surely by now deserved by Choi), the abbot – a man named Watanabe – knew the founder of the martial art *daito-ryu aiki-jujitsu*, Takeda Sokaku.

By all accounts, Choi was next whisked by Sokaku to a *dōjō* on Shin Shu mountain, where he and his *sensei* lived and trained for the following thirty years. During this time, said Choi later, he grew to have a complete understanding of Sokaku's style.

Following the end of the Second World War, Choi returned to Korea, where for a time he earned his living raising and selling pigs. However, a local brewery chairman happened to see him in action when a heated discussion he'd been having with several men turned ugly. In the ensuing skirmish, Choi quickly saw the men off.

'Hey, you're pretty good,' said the brewery chairman, a man named Suh Bok Sub (who was himself a first *dan* in *judō*). 'Why don't I pay to have a *dojang* (the Korean for training hall) built on my premises, so that you can teach there? I can be your first pupil!'

And so it was; in 1951 the two men opened a school named the Korean Yu Kwan Sool Hapki Dojang, followed, in 1958, by Choi's very own school – which for the first time bore the shortened title 'Hapkido'.

Having travelled as far as North America to teach his new martial art, Choi died in 1986 at the age of eighty-two.

CHOU, SENG

Seng Chou (480–560 AD) was feeble, slightly-built, and often bullied by the other monks who were resident at the Shaolin Temple. Greatly peeved by all of this, Seng Chou went one night into the Temple's great hall, where there stood before him a massive statue of the Buddhist military god Jingangshen.

'If you can hear me, great one,' whispered Seng Chou in prayer, 'please help me. Make me strong, and big, so that I can defend myself when next the other monks chide me.'

This continued for several further nights, with Seng Chou praying alone to the fearsome-looking statue. Finally, after almost a week had passed, Seng Chou's prayers were answered.

'What's the matter with you, mouse?' mocked Jingangshen in great, booming tones, suddenly appearing in his divine form before the cowering monk.

'The other monks are always mocking me – they call

me weak, and useless,' protested Seng Chou in a faltering voice, wholly unable to meet the god's fiery gaze.

'But you *are* weak, and you *are* useless!' laughed the god, swiping Seng Chou around the head. It was the mildest of blows, and yet it knocked the monk flying.

'I know I am,' nodded Seng Chou as he picked himself up slowly off the floor, tears appearing. 'That's why I need your help to change.'

So obvious was his misery that Jingangshen felt something stir in his otherwise hardened heart.

'So be it,' said the god solemnly.

'You'll … you'll help me?' stammered Seng Chou, wiping his eyes.

'In a way,' answered Jingangshen cryptically. 'But first you must help yourself.'

'How do you mean, master?' the monk wanted to know.

'You must eat flesh.'

Seng Chou recoiled as though stung.

'Master,' he said breathlessly, 'you must know that it is forbidden for a monk to eat the meat of any creature. That is a sacred commandment to us.'

'Eat flesh,' shrugged Jingangshen, 'or be damned all your life. There is no other way.'

'I … I cannot,' Seng Chou said miserably. 'You ask too much.'

At once a great blade appeared in one of the god's hands, its blade pressed against the monk's throat. In the god's other hand was a great sinewy lump of meat.

'Eat this,' said Jingangshen, 'or die by this blade. You asked me for help, and now you must accept what I tell you. There is no other way, except for that of death.'

Hesitatingly, Seng Chou reached out for the meat. He felt sick to the stomach as he began to chew – and yet it tasted considerably better than he'd expected.

And all at once he felt a warm glow start in his arms, legs, and chest. Suddenly he realised that he was stood at least a foot taller than he had before, and he looked gratefully at Jingangshen.

'I have granted your wish,' said the god, the meat and sword now absent. 'Never trouble me again.'

And with that, all that remained was the statue with its fixed, fathomless gaze.

Dawn was breaking as Seng Chou returned to the dormitory he shared with the other monks. They were starting to awaken, yawning and washing with the aid of a water jug as they prepared themselves for the morning's prayers.

'Seng Chou, you little maggot, where have you be – '

The usual tirade of abuse stopped the moment the monks took notice of the fact that Seng Chou was a good foot taller than he'd stood before, and that his arms and legs were now like tree trunks.

'Never mock me again,' said the monk quietly. 'Do you understand?'

'Yes, yes,' said the other monks together, wondering just how such a transformation could have occurred overnight. They knew better than to ask, however.

From that moment on Seng Chou became one of the Shaolin Temple's most skilled martial (fighting) monks. He was fond of jumping onto rooftops and lifting great weights, while his friend Hui Guang (who hadn't been given any special powers by Jingangshen) could apparently kick a shuttlecock 500 consecutive times with his feet while stood on a thin iron beam suspended several feet in the air.

CONSTERDINE, PETER

One name consistently mentioned by such premier British martial artists as Kevin O'Hagan, Brian Seabright and **Geoff Thompson** is Peter Consterdine's. From the age of fifteen he has been a practitioner of many different martial arts, including *karate* (in which he is currently ranked seventh *dan*, and a former England International) and *Wing Chun kung-fu*, Consterdine also honed his fighting skills in the decade he spent working 'on the door' of some of Manchester's roughest nightclubs.

Like **Geoff Thompson** (with whom he is joint Chief Instructor of the British Combat Association), Consterdine's 'real-life' experiences of violence have led him to reject a great deal of what is traditionally taught in the *dōjō*. So many techniques look good in practise, but are (to quote **Geoff Thompson**) 'about as much use as a chocolate kettle' if they are ever used in a real self-defence situation.

Through his lectures, lessons, and videos (one of which, based upon Consterdine's reputation as being one of the world's hardest hitters, is entitled *Power-strike*), Consterdine instead shows techniques that have been fully tried and tested in what he refers to as the 'Pavement Arena'. As a much called-upon bodyguard and security advisor (his clients having included a number of UK police forces), Consterdine's work has taken him to some of the most troubled parts of the globe, and few would doubt his credentials when it comes to teaching authentic self-defence.

D

DOLMAN, CHRIS

Born in the Netherlands in 1945, Chris Dolman has been described by the 'Dutch Animal' **Jon Bluming** as being '... the best all-round student I ever had'. At the age of twenty-four he became World Champion at Sambo, in Moscow, effectively beating the Russians at their own sport, and went on to win numerous medals in the world of 'freefighting' – which is, as the name suggests, a tournament where expert practitioners of various styles thrash it out to determine who's best. For a time Dolman, like **Bluming**, was involved in providing security for the clubs and casinos in Amsterdam's red-light district, but now he is currently busy training new fighting talent.

DONG, FAN XU

A giant of a man, weighing in at around 300 pounds, Fan Xu Dong was also a master of Wong Long's 'Praying Mantis' style of *kung-fu*. So expert was he at fighting, and so strong, that it is said he once killed two bulls who tried to attack him as he strolled across a field.

He became a hero when he slew a Japanese samurai warrior who was making his way slowly across China, challenging and killing any Chinese swordsman who happened to be in his path.

Dong had his own challenge instantly accepted by the samurai, who the following morning found himself being sliced in half from the groin upwards.

DONG, HAICHUAN

The founder of *baguazhang* ('eight shaped palm boxing') – one of the three major internal Chinese martial arts – Dong Haichuan was born in Zhu village sometime around the late seventeenth or early eighteenth century. From childhood he trained in a variety of martial arts, and as a young man was frequently in trouble due to his love of fighting.

He then went travelling around China, often so poor that he had to beg for food but always practising his martial arts daily. He finally obtained employment as a tax collector in Mongolia, where he stayed for around a decade.

After that he set himself up as a full-time martial arts' instructor, accepting students for his style of *baguazhang*. However, some people still needed persuading that Dong was any good. Like **Guo Yunshen**, an exponent of *Xingyiquan* (one of the other three major Chinese martial arts along with *Taijiquan*) whose 'divine crushing fist' had killed at least one fighter.

Yunshen confidently challenged the much older Dong, and the two men fought – for days, some sources say. At last Dong gained the upper hand, but both men had by then formed a mutual admiration for one another.

Dong Haichuan seems to have had a particularly forgiving nature. A tale is told of how he once disarmed a would-be assassin of a pistol while pretending to be asleep. The assassin fell to his knees, begging first for his life and then to be taken on as a student. By all accounts, Dong spared the former and consented to the latter.

DRAEGER, DONALD 'DONN' FREDERICK

Draeger was instrumental in continuing the science of 'hoplology' – the study of human combative performance and behaviour (the word derived from the Greek *hoplon,* meaning 'armed' or 'armoured') – that was first developed by Sir Richard Francis Burton.

Along with such men as **Jon Bluming** and martial arts' historian **Robert W. Smith**, Draeger was particularly notable for introducing Eastern martial arts to the Western world.

Born in 1922 in Milwaukee, Wisconsin, USA, Draeger began learning *jujitsu* when just seven years of age, later taking in interest in *judō*. (He would be instrumental in founding the Amateur Judō Association – America's first national *judō* body.)

The Second World War saw Draeger promoted to the rank of Major, and a posting to the Pacific Rim allowed him to train with many Eastern martial arts' masters.

His height – 6 foot 2 inches – and weight – around 200 pounds – meant that he was particularly suited to grappling arts such as *judō,* although he would conduct extensive studies into such striking styles as the '**Mas' Oyama** school of *karate*, as well as becoming expert at many different types of weaponry.

Draeger was an extremely intellectual and well-read man, with a broad range of interests (not just martial arts – engineering and cultural studies were of equal interest to him). With a well-developed air of charm, he was able to convince the most reluctant of Eastern masters to show this young foreigner the secrets of their martial art.

Another trick of Draeger's was to go with some other Westerners into a remote area, perhaps a backwater village, and to start training in full view of a local coffee shop. Soon enough someone watching would say that they 'did something like that', and would show Draeger their art form.

Draeger lived for many years in Japan (where he spent several weeks each year training top swordsmen at a remote mountain retreat), but also spent time in India, Sri Lanka, Mongolia, China, Taiwan, Korea, Hong Kong, Malaysia and Indonesia, all the while absorbing and documenting whatever fighting styles he happened to come across. In the process of doing this, it's claimed, he eventually garnered over 100 black belts in different martial arts.

Draeger wrote extensively about the martial arts, publishing numerous books including *Comprehensive Asian Fighting Arts*, co-written with his long-term friend and colleague, **Robert W. Smith**. He served as a martial arts' advisor on the set of the James Bond film *You Only Live Twice*, where he was also obliged to act as a stunt double for Sean Connery.

Throughout his later life, Draeger conducted extensive 'field trips' through Asia each year, and it was during one such trip that he contracted severe amoebic dysentery while on the Indonesian island of Sumatra.

While hospitalised, it was discovered that Draeger had cancer of the liver and intestines, his pain made even worse by severely swollen legs. Attempts at treatment failed, and Draeger died on 20 October, 1982.

Perhaps the highest testament to Draeger's talents comes from **Jon Bluming**, who has described him as 'Japan's first foreign Samurai'. And as **Robert W. Smith** wrote in his book, *Martial Musings*: '... Hear his name. Donn Draeger: don't nod in recognition; Donn Draeger: bow with admiration and respect ...'

D'TOM, NAI KHANOM

A warrior and *Muay Thai* fighter who was imprisoned as a slave labourer in Burma, D'tom was given a choice: remain a prisoner, or fight a man of his captors' choice and (should he win) secure his freedom.

'I'll fight whoever you choose,' said D'tom defiantly.

'Good,' said his captors. 'And by the way, the man we have in mind is considered Burma's finest fighter.'

In spite of this, D'tom beat his opponent – and the other eleven men who followed, all of them desperate to put this slave labourer down.

'Excellent, excellent,' said the Burmese King Mangra at last; for he'd been watching the entire performance. 'Every part of you is blessed with venom. Even with just your bare hands, you can fell any number of opponents.'

Bloody and out of breath, D'tom nodded and bowed.

'Thank you, your Majesty,' he said.

'And now for your reward,' said King Mangra. 'You may take gold and jewels – or a choice of Siamese women captured during battle between Burma and Siam.' (Siam being the old name for Thailand.)

'I take the women,' said D'tom, 'so that I may give them their freedom.'

'As you wish,' said the king, motioning for a courtier to bring the women forward.

Over 200 years have passed, but still D'tom's victory is celebrated every year in Thailand, on March 17, as National *Muay Thai* Day.

E

EMELIANENKO, FEODOR VLADIMIROVICH

Commonly referred to as 'Fedor', Emelianenko (born 28 September, 1976, in Russia's Rubeshnoe Lugansk region) is one of the best-known heavyweight fighters in the world of mixed martial arts. A former firefighter, serving with the Russian military from 1995–1997, he began training early on with *judō* and *Sambo* (in both of which he was declared the 1997 Russian National Champion) before expanding his fighting arsenal through such 'striking' arts as *Muay Thai* kickboxing.

Six feet tall and weighing in at around 230 pounds, Emelianenko's nicknames include 'The Terminator' and 'The Cyborg'. His 'ground and pound' technique – taking an opponent to the floor with a throw, and then hammering them with his fists at the same time as he looks to apply a submission hold – is widely feared, and only once in his mixed martial arts' career has he been defeated. This followed a controversial stoppage in late 2000 by a ringside doctor, after Emelianenko's forehead was sliced open by an illegal (but also accidental) elbow strike from his opponent, the Japanese fighter Tsuyoshi 'TK' Kohsaka.

Outside of the ring, Emelianenko appears to be a refreshingly down-to-earth individual, who once stated that he began a fighting career because he '... didn't have any money'. He was born to an impoverished family, who for a time lived in a single room with Emelianenko's mother – a teacher – growing vegetables on a nearby plot of land when there was not enough money to buy food. An often sickly child who was obliged to share an overcoat with his brother, Emelianenko went on to become a fighter who earned an estimated $1.5 million for a fight in Saitama, Japan on 31 December, 2007. (Emelianenko took less than two minutes to secure victory with an arm-bar.)

F

FAIRBAIRN, WILLIAM E.

Born in 1885, William E. Fairbairn's experiences in the Royal Marine Light Infantry, and then the Shanghai Municipal Police (whom he joined in 1907) led him to develop his own form of hand-to-hand combat, which he called 'Defendu'. Based upon *jujitsu* and such Chinese martial arts as *kung-fu*, it also featured brutally efficient techniques that Fairbairn had developed in the countless 'one-on-one' fights he'd had whilst serving as a police officer. (Some estimates state that there were over 600 such altercations.)

Fairbairn also concentrated on studying and developing weaponry (techniques as well as equipment), and lent his name to the famous double-edged 'Fairbairn–Sykes fighting knife' that became standard issue for

British Commandos during the Second World War, and which continues to remain in production.

Rumoured to have been the inspiration for Ian Fleming's character, James Bond, Fairbairn died in 1960.

FILIPOVIÇ, MIRKO 'CRO COP'

Born on 10 September, 1974, Filipoviç won the PRIDE 2006 Open Weight Grand Prix on his thirty-second birthday. A kickboxer, Filipoviç is particularly feared for his lightning left high kick, which has felled many an opponent. His nickname, 'Cro Cop', is short for 'Croatian Cop' – Filipoviç was a member of Croatia's elite anti-terrorist unit ATJ Luãko for six years. He has since pursued a minor acting career, and was from 2003–2007 a member of the Croatian Parliament.

FUJIBAYASHI, SABUJI

A seventeenth-century *ninja*, Sabuji Fujibayashi is popularly believed to have been the author of the *'ninja* training manual' the *Bansenshukai* (commonly translated as either 'Sea of Myriad Rivers Merging' or 'Ten Thousand Rivers Flow into the Sea'). Chapters within the *Bansenshukai* – which it is claimed Fujibayashi wrote in 1676 – concentrate on weaponry, astronomy, philosophy, military history, and so on. One section dispenses advice on how a *ninja* may best disguise himself before undertaking a mission, declaring that by cutting one's hair in a 'moon shape' (whatever that may be) a man may '... appear like a woman'.

Following the end of the Second World War, hand-written copies of the *Bansenshukai* were, for a short time, made available to the Japanese public, presumably in a bid to bolster general moral during the American occupation of Japan. It is remarkable that such a document was even written in the first place, as *ninja* commonly preferred to shroud their knowledge and techniques in mystery, delighting in common misconceptions (for example, suggestions that they could fly or breathe underwater), and passing on what they knew only to trusted students in conditions of absolute secrecy.

At the time of writing this book is not in print, although it can be found – in both Japanese and English – on the internet.

FUNAKOSHI, GICHIN

Funakoshi was the founder of *Shotokan karate*, created when he merged together the two styles of *karate* he'd been taught from boyhood on the island of Okinawa. He was a weak and sickly child (as seems to be the norm for many a martial arts' master), and as a curious form of 'medicine' a local doctor prescribed him *karate* lessons, along with some special healing herbs.

In 1917, Funakoshi was asked to demonstrate his martial art in Japan, at an exhibition organised by the

Ministry of Education. Funakoshi's skill at this point was so great that it was said he'd faced a man with a sword and won the ensuing skirmish.

He was asked back a second time, in 1922, and then again to give a special performance in front of the Emperor and the royal family. It was after this that Funakoshi decided to remain in Japan.

Funakoshi remained a particularly quiet and humble man right up until his death, aged eighty-nine. It was said that he only ever had one 'real' (i.e. outside of the *dōjō*) fight in his life; when a thief tried to attack him. On that occasion, Funakoshi quickly seized the unfortunate man by his testicles and held him like that until a police officer walked by. Forever afterwards, however, Funakoshi agonised over whether he'd used too much force.

G

GEESINK, ANTONIUS 'ANTON'

Born in Holland in 1934, Geesink destroyed Japan's hope – indeed virtual expectation – of taking all four gold medals in *judō* (in the lightweight–open-weight categories) at the 1964 Tokyo Olympics. All across the host country, grown men huddled around precious television sets (these were the first televised Olympics) and literally wept as Geesink defeated Akio Kaminaga by using *kesa-gatame* – a ground hold which, when applied properly by an opponent such as the 130 kilogramme, 6-foot-7-inch Geesink, is almost impossible to escape. (It seemed to be of no consolation to the Japanese that they had been victorious in the light-, middle- and heavyweight categories and had lost only one gold medal in *judō* – Geesink and Kaminaga having competed in the open-weight division.)

Kaminaga was lambasted throughout Japan for his defeat, but chose not to follow the actions of two other Japanese athletes (a runner and hurdler), who'd committed suicide following their 'failure' to perform as had been expected. A grudging respect was also given to Geesink by the Japanese when the Dutchman, following his victory, angrily waved away an attempted 'mat invasion' by some of his own countrymen – something which was seen to have preserved *judō*'s 'decorum'.

Geesink is today ranked tenth *dan* in *judō* – the highest grading it is possible to receive.

GRACEFFO, ANTONIO

An adventure travel writer and martial artist (and prior to 9/11 an investment banker working on Wall Street), Antonio Graceffo wrote about his experiences studying *kung-fu* at China's *Shaolin* Temple – not one of its numerous satellite 'schools', where most foreigners can expect to train – in *The Monk from Brooklyn.*

It is a detailed diary that does not pull any punches; Graceffo seems almost fond, for example, of frequently reminding his reader of the less-than-sanitary conditions in which the monks live, and of the technologically backward and generally restrictive Chinese way of life.

Graceffo is also not afraid to show how he frequently provokes confrontation. When a *Shaolin* instructor 'backs down' to him, following a thinly-veiled challenge by the American that they fight for real (Graceffo had been angered by the instructor's apparent bullying of a child student), the Brooklyn-born Graceffo concludes that the man has thus become his 'bitch'.

As an insight into a centuries' old way of life, however, training with men who have near superhuman physical abilities, *The Monk from Brooklyn* is compelling. (Graceffo has also studied *Muay Thai* kickboxing in Thailand, and frequently contributes articles detailing his experiences to such martial arts' publications as *Black Belt*.)

GRACIE, CARLOS

'... If you want to get your face beaten and well smashed, your ass kicked and arms broken, contact Carlos Gracie at this address ...'

The above, delicately-worded advertisement ran in a Brazilian newspaper during the mid-1920s. It came from Carlos Gracie, who would become the founder of the world-famous 'Gracie' school of *jujitsu*, considered by many to be one of the most comprehensive fighting systems ever developed.

But the story really starts in the late 1800s in Japan, when a man called Mitsuyo Maeda – who would later become better known as 'Count Koma' – switched from learning classical *jujitsu* to the developing art of *judō*, all the while observed by *judō*'s founder **Jigoro Kano**.

Kano thought his 5-foot 6-inch, 150-pound student was good – in fact a virtual prodigy – although he was still a little too fond of drinking *sake* and indulging in fisticuffs in the street.

'He needs focus, a direction,' considered Kano, who, in 1904, thus ordered Maeda to go to America and start spreading the word about *judō*.

Once in the United States, Maeda took on a series of challenges against sporting jocks, including a much larger man who had the bowel-loosening title of 'The Butcher'. But Maeda bested everyone he was put against, meeting raw brawn with superior technique and lightening speed.

He then travelled extensively (including visiting Europe, and it was when he was in Spain that he earned the nickname 'Count Koma'), until finally he was requested by the Japanese government to help found a colony in northern Brazil.

He was greatly assisted in this matter by an official named Gasto Gracie, who also showed a lot of interest in Count Koma's martial art. In return for Gracie's help, therefore, Koma agreed to show Gracie's frail, 15-year-old son Carlos a little of what he knew.

Even the descendants of Carlo Gracie themselves are a little unsure of exactly how long Carlos studied with Koma. Certainly it was for longer than two years, though no more than five. What is known is that Carlos studied everything from devastating elbow strikes and knee blows right through to a multitude of submission techniques when fighting 'went to ground'. (A place where the Gracie brothers retain their superiority to this day.)

Aged nineteen, fully trained and feeling rather confident, Carlos Gracie moved to Rio de Janeiro to teach and compete in martial arts. He said goodbye to his Japanese teacher, who left to embark on yet another bout of travelling and generally disappear from this story.

In Rio de Janeiro, Gracie opened his 'Academia Gracie de *jujitsu*', somehow managing to attract students despite his fairly 'forceful' way of advertising (see start of entry). He also shared what he knew with his brothers, and, ultimately, with eleven of his twenty-one children. Between them, the Gracies pioneered – and continue to promulgate – a system of fighting that to this day dominates 'no-rules' contests around the world.

Ju-jitsu is not just about fighting, say the Gracies. It is a system of life, a way of respecting yourself and others, of creating a healthy mind and body. It advocates the 'Gracie diet', with alcohol, tobacco, and any kind of drug, being strictly forbidden.

'Follow the Gracie style of *jujitsu*', say 'today's' Gracies, such as Carlos Jr., and you will be rewarded with a sense of well-being that is otherwise hard to attain in today's hectic world.

GREAT, ALEXANDER THE

Whilst a popular point of view is that all Asian martial arts have their origins in India, there are some who suggest that we can actually look even further back: in fact to the time of Alexander the Great (356–323 BC), whose invasion of India is sometimes credited with having given that country the so-called 'first mixed martial art' of *pankration* (meaning 'all strength' or 'all power').

Introduced as an Olympic sport in Greece in 648 BC, *pankration* combined boxing with grappling. Its practitioners were shackled with very few rules; they were only forbidden to bite or gouge each others' eyes out. Two men might fight naked for hours until sunset, or until one of them either signalled defeat or died – whichever came soonest.

A Greek athlete named Dioxippus – who was closely acquainted with Alexander the Great – is generally considered to have been the finest *pankratiast*. In 336 BC, he became the Olympic champion by default when no other man dared to fight him.

Another fighter reportedly broke his opponent's fingers in a bid to free himself from a stranglehold. The opponent shrieked with pain and signalled defeat – but after the first man had been declared the winner, it was discovered that the strangle had, in fact, ultimately killed him. Still, he was permitted to retain the title of victor. (Something which no doubt proved of great consolation.)

A less lethal – but still fully effective – form of *pankration* continues to be practised to this day, with its leading teacher 'Aris Makris' having served as an advisor for the fight scenes in the hit Spartan-warrior movie *300* (2007). (Another modern-day *pankratiast*, Demitrios 'Jim' Arvanitis – who is himself of Spartan-Greek descent – is frequently referred to as *pankration*'s 'Renaissance Man'.)

GUAN, SHUEN

During China's Jin Dynasty, a village was attacked by bandits. Only one person – and a 13-year-old girl at that – was able to fight her way through the invading horde using a spear, a sword, and, when these failed her, her bare fists and feet.

Time and time again the bandits tried to cut her down, yet finally she got through to the next village and a general there called Sheh Lan.

'Please, come quickly!' pleaded the teenage girl, who was panting heavily and had several bleeding wounds. 'My village is being attacked!'

Spurred into action, the general gathered his men

and, taking Shuen Guan with him, made his way to the stricken village. There, a pitched battle took place between the soldiers and the bandits, with the bandits eventually forced to flee.

'Thank you! Thank you so much!' said the villagers as one.

'You would have done better to have followed this young girl's example – to have tried to fight for your homes,' said Sheh Lan severely to the cowering populace, who meekly nodded their understanding and forever afterwards treated Shuen Guan as a hero.

Indeed, so impressed was the Emperor of China by the tale of her bravery that it's said he nicknamed her 'The Little Tigress'. For her part, Shuen Guan continued to practise unarmed combat and weapon forms, soon becoming an expert *sifu,* or 'teacher'.

GUO, YUNSHEN

Born in 1822, Guo Yunshen was a noted practitioner of *xingyiquan*, one of China's three most prominent 'internal' styles – the other two being *tai chi chuan* and *baguazhang*.

In his younger years, Guo was something of a violent character, who endlessly practised his *Beng Quan* (what is basically a punch). So proficient did he become at this particular move that he killed at least one man with it, and as a result was sent to prison for three years where he spent much of his time manacled to a cell wall.

Not to be discouraged, however, with his free hand he continued to endlessly practise his Beng Quan, and upon his release was so well known for it that he was called (deep breath) 'Half-step Crushing Fist Strikes Everywhere Under Heaven'.

Guo is rumoured to have fought for anything up to a number of days with **Dong Haichuan,** the founder of *baguazhang*, who was apparently not put off by Guo's nickname (which had become shortened to a more wieldy, though no less scary, 'Divine Crushing Fist'). **Dong Haichuan** eventually won, but both men were left with a mutual respect for one another.

In his later years, Guo mellowed significantly but remained a firm believer in a martial artist learning a few movements well, rather than a lot of movements badly.

H

HAN, BONG-SOO

Han Bong-Soo was born in 1933 in South Korea. He began his martial arts' training with *karate*, and had obtained a black belt by the time he was introduced to *hapkido* – the Korean martial art innovated by Choi Yong Sul.

Han was instantly hooked, and in the late 1960s he moved to America, opening his own *hapkido dojang* (training hall) in a rough area of Los Angeles. From initially struggling to find students, and working days in a factory in an attempt to make ends meet, Han Bong-Soo would go on to appear in a number of movies (such as 1977's comedy *The Kentucky Fried Movie*, which featured Han in a spoof of **Bruce Lee**'s *Enter the Dragon* entitled *A Fistful of Yen*), and generally become so well-known for his martial arts expertise that he was ultimately referred to as the 'Father of Hapkido'. (He was inducted into *Black Belt* magazine's 'Hall of Fame' in 1978.) Han, meanwhile, was always at pains to point out that martial arts' training should primarily be focused towards developing an individual's mental and physical well-being – the ability to fight, he added, was of the least importance.

Having achieved the outstanding rank of ninth *dan* in his martial discipline, and having been both the founder and President of the International Hapkido Federation since 1974, Han Bong-Soo passed away in early 2007.

HANGAKU, 'LADY'

Samurai history does not exactly abound with stories of female warriors, however, one of the few exceptions concerns the twelfth-century 'Lady' Hangaku (also often referred to as Itagaki). Descriptions concerning her appearance have doubtless been embellished over the years: she was apparently 'strong as a man', and yet also exquisitely beautiful – indeed, something of a supermodel of her age. Commanding an army of some 3 000 men, she excelled in the use of the bow and arrow, and also the *naginata*. This is a long pole with a curved blade at its end; traditionally, women were instructed in its use, so that they had some means of defending themselves if they were attacked while their husbands, brothers, or fathers were away. The *naginata*'s length allowed a woman to keep her distance from her attacker, who was likely to be both male and superior in strength.

In any case, history records that Lady Hangaku was finally defeated during battle and brought, severely wounded, before her captors. One such captor, however, was so overwhelmed by her aforementioned strength and beauty that he ended up marrying her. And in finest storytelling tradition, everyone lived happily ever after. (Another, less romantic ending, however, merely has Lady Hangaku dying from her injuries.)

HATTORI, HANZO

Born in Japan in 1541, Hattori was, from childhood, trained in the ways of *ninjutsu*, and by his late teens he was particularly expert in the use of the spear. Passionately devoted to his master, the future first Shogun of Japan, Tokugawa Ieyasu, he was nicknamed 'Devil Hanzo' for his fighting skill. (He was also known as 'Hanzo of the Spear', for obvious reasons.) It was even rumoured that he could disappear from one room and reappear in another, or hold his breath underwater for any length of time.

Hattori, who has been immortalised in an array of novels, films and comics, died in 1596 – either from natural causes or at the hands of another *ninja*, depending on which source you choose to believe. His remains lie at Sainen-ji Temple in Shinjuku, Tokyo.

HIGAONNA, KANRYO

'His hands and feet moved faster than lightning ... the severity of the training he underwent in China is beyond comprehension ...'

So said one of Grandmaster Higaonna's students, in celebration of a man who, in 1869 and at the age of sixteen, travelled from Okinawa, Japan, to China, to find a martial arts' master who was prepared to teach him.

He finally found one in Ryu Ryu Ko, Higaonna becoming this man's *uchi deshi* or 'private disciple' after Higaonna saved Ko's daughter from drowning during a flood. (For several years before this, Ko had apparently been satisfied for Higaonna to merely do chores around his home, repeatedly ignoring Higaonna's pleas that he be taken on as a student.)

In the thirteen or so years (estimates do vary) that Higaonna stayed in China, he became an expert in numerous martial arts – including those that utilised weapons – and was also trained as a healer, learning how to treat people's various afflictions with a variety of herbs.

Finally he left China and returned to Okinawa to

show the populace there what he had learnt. Those people he accepted as students were shocked at the change in his character: quiet, indeed almost meek, in everyday life, Higaonna became like a tiger in the *dōjō*, demanding that his students give their utmost physical effort at all times.

Many found that they couldn't stand such training and quit, though those that stuck with it went on to reap the rewards that came from being taught by a master. In awe and admiration, they bestowed upon their *sensei*, or 'teacher', the name *kensei* – 'sacred fists'.

HISAMORI, TENENUCHI

Exactly when, where and how the martial art that we loosely refer to as *jujitsu* arose is a matter of some conjecture amongst martial art aficionados.

But if (as is often claimed) a man named Tenenuchi Hisamori didn't actually *found* this particular martial art, he did at least significantly helped its development, establishing a *jujitsu* school in 1533 that specialised in both armed and unarmed fighting techniques.

HOOD, ROBIN

Well, why not? Robin Hood was, by all accounts, a master archer, swordsman, wrestler, highly skilled with a stave and, presumably, no slouch with his fists, either.

In other words: an expert practitioner of traditional English martial arts.

He is variously described as having lived in the eleventh, twelfth and thirteenth centuries (i.e. – take your pick); and as for his name, one explanation concerns it being an adaptation of the words 'robbing hood'. This refers to the hooded outlaw who had a penchant for relieving fat priests and noblemen of their bulging purses at knifepoint.

As likely as not the many stories concerning 'Robin Hood' are embellished myths concerning any number of different men, although we like to think of just one, happy-go-lucky hero scoffing the Sheriff's venison and generally thumbing his nose at authority in general.

However, some evidence points to the fact that this jolly character, clad entirely in Lincoln green and with a pure heart that permitted no foul play, may actually have had a darker side.

Stories abound concerning his run-ins with his nemesis, Sir Guy of Gisbourne – although less reported is the claim that when Robin finally succeeded in slaying the man, he proceeded to stick Gisbourne's rotting head on top of his bow.

So what made Robin abandon normal thirteenth-century (or whenever) peasant life in the first place? At what point did he say to himself: 'Bugger this – I'm done with tending to my small field and those couple of pigs. Keep the dismal one-roomed hut, keep the staple diet of black bread and cheese – I'm going to disappear into Sherwood Forest, take up with a bunch of characters with names like Friar Tuck and Little John, and generally become a bit of a hell-raiser.'

Once again, there are a number of different explanations. One details how Robin merely got a bit bored ploughing his field and tending to his swine and decided to live a more exciting life, while another details how he was forced to flee when he was caught killing the Sheriff's dear.

Sentenced to have his right hand amputated for this crime, Robin instead slipped away into the forest, with a price immediately being put on his head.

There he lived out his days drinking, causing mischief, trying to get intimate with Maid Marian, and generally having a right old good time. How (and when) he died is yet another source of conjecture, although one story details how, following injuries caused by a 20-foot drop onto stone, he 'bled' excessively, and so fatally weakened.

Knowing the end was near, he summoned all his remaining strength and shot an arrow out of the window of the room in which he was resting, demanding that he be buried wherever the arrow landed.

HUA, MULAN

Hua Mulan is the legendary Chinese heroine who was immortalised in Disney's 1998 animated film called (wait for it ...) *Mulan. Mulan* was just the latest in a long line of embellishments to a story that is estimated to be around 1300 years old.

In fact, the tale of Mulan started life as a poem called 'The Ballad of Mulan', or 'Ode to Mulan', taken from an ancient collection of Chinese ballads and songs entitled *Yue-fu,* and written some time during the Tang Dynasty (think sixth century).

Mulan's father is summoned by the Emperor (referred to in the poem as 'the Khan') to go and fight in Northern China. The father is, however, somewhat old and infirm, which causes Mulan to abandon her weaving and instead dress as a man and go in his place. The poem describes how she hurriedly visits various markets to buy a number of items for her horse and herself.

She leaves Song (her village in eastern Henan Province) and travels '10 000 miles in the war machine', conducting herself with such aplomb on the battlefield that the Khan himself offers her a government post; a reward for her years of military service.

'Actually,' says Mulan humbly, 'I'd rather just return home.'

'As you wish,' shrugs the Khan.

Later, Mulan's comrades come to visit her and are shocked to discover that this brave warrior they knew on the battlefield is in fact female. The poem ends by demanding how the casual onlooker can possibly determine the sexes of two rabbits or hares that are 'running close to the ground'. A way of saying, no doubt, that in the heat of battle there is zero difference between a female warrior and a male.

HUNG, SAMMO

Born in 1952 in Hong Kong, and largely raised by his grandparents (his grandmother, Chin Tsi-ang or 'Mama Hung', was herself a well-known actress and martial artist who died just two years short of her 100th birthday, in 2007), Sammo Hung attended the infamous Peking Opera School from the age of nine. Here, students spent up to eighteen hours a day learning such skills as acrobatics, martial arts, singing, and dancing; all of which were intended to serve their future career 'on the stage'. One of Hung's peers at the school was a boy named Chan Kong-sang, who would go on to achieve worldwide fame as **Jackie Chan**. (Hung and Chan first appeared together in the 1962 movie *Big and Little Wong Tin Bar*, of which there is, unfortunately, no known copy remaining. Along with fellow actor and martial artist Yuen Biao, Hung and Chan have appeared in a number of films since – such as *Dragons Forever*, in 1988 – with the trio popularly referred to as the 'three brothers'.)

As Hung entered adulthood he starred in a string of fast-paced martial arts' flicks which, like Jackie Chan's creations, frequently contained a distinct element of comedy. He also appeared in *Enter the Dragon*, in 1972, as the *Shaolin* student whom **Bruce Lee** defeats early on in the movie. (In 1979, after Lee's death, Hung starred in the 'comic' *Enter the Fat Dragon*, the title a reference to Hung's portly physique. In it Hung plays a pig farmer who idolises **Bruce Lee**.) During the early 1980s, Hung helped innovate the popular *Jiang Shi* or 'hopping vampire' genre, in which ancient Chinese spells and *kung-fu* are necessary to subdue the bouncing ghouls. (For example, *The Dead and the Deadly* in 1982.)

Martial Law (a series produced by US television network CBS between 1998 and 2000) proved a surprise hit for Hung, who played a Chinese policeman working in Los Angeles. (Western audiences were amazed that someone of Hung's size could still be so obviously agile. They were also intrigued by the ugly circular scar that Hung has just above his top lip – the result of a street fight in Hung's youth that saw his adversary push a broken bottle into his face.) Hung continues to act, and also works extensively as a fight choreographer, stunt co-ordinator, director, producer, and writer.

HUO, YUANJIA

Born in 1868, Huo Yuanjia was a sickly child who was troubled by a variety of ailments, including jaundice.

(This would periodically re-occur throughout his life.) Consequently, Huo's father – who was both a farmer as well as a bodyguard of wealthy merchants – forbade his son from following family tradition of practising *wushu* (Chinese martial arts), instead demanding that he devote himself to more scholarly pursuits.

The young Yuanjia, however, secretly watched his family train at night. (Yuanjia was but one of ten children, most of whom received tuition in the martial arts from their father), later to practise – again in secret – all he'd observed. Slowly, over many years, he became an expert martial artist. Finally, when he was aged around twenty-two, he astounded everyone who knew him by soundly beating a hoodlum who'd been tormenting his brother. This caused a number of other fighters in the area to challenge Huo, who subsequently bested everyone he fought. Quickly, his reputation began to spread.

At this stage in its history, China was being crippled by a succession of natural disasters, including floods and famines, chronic opium addiction amongst its populace, and what almost amounted to a 'carving up' of the country by England, France, Russia, Germany, and Japan. To add insult to injury, a Russian wrestler currently in China was loudly declaring that he could beat any Chinaman who cared to fight him. The Chinese were, he declared, the '... weak men of the East'.

In the 2006 film *Fearless*, which stars **Jet Li** in a highly fictionalised portrayal of Huo Yuanjia's life (although the story of Huo Yuanjia has, indeed, become so exaggerated over the years that it is often difficult to separate fact from fiction), Huo fights four foreigners in one day in a bid to prove that *wushu* is supreme. (*Fearless* is just one of several films that have been based upon the exploits of one of China's most popular heroes.)

But, in reality, although Huo *did* challenge the Russian wrestler to a fight, along with an English boxer named Hercules O'Brien. Both men declined to participate. In fact, at Huo's demand, the Russian wrestler even wrote an apology for his comments, which was printed in a major newspaper. However, Huo and a few of his students did have an altercation with some Japanese *judoka*, most of whom (the *judoka*, that is) sustained broken hands in the brawl.

When the unpopular Manchu Emperor banned martial arts, fearing that it could possibly be used in an uprising against him, Huo Yuanjia nevertheless opened a *wushu* training school which he disguised with the title 'Chin Woo Physical Training Centre'. (The Chin Woo Association continues to flourish today, with branches in many different countries.)

Huo, however, was steadily sickening with another attack of jaundice – from which he suffered so frequently that he'd become known as the 'Yellow-faced Tiger' – as well as tuberculosis, and died, aged forty-two, on 9 August, 1910.

Rumour quickly spread that he'd been poisoned by the Japanese (as is portrayed in *Fearless*), though it's possible that the attempted treatment of his diseases in fact resulted in his death. Almost eighty years later, his bones were analysed and found to contain the black spots symptomatic of arsenic poisoning. In the early 1900s, however, arsenic was commonly used to treat TB; so the mystery that continues to surround Huo Yuanjia's early death only adds to his legend.

HWANG, JANG-LEE

Born in 1944 and a ninth *dan* black belt in *tae kwon do*, Hwang Jang-Lee bears the title 'Grandmaster'. A film star as well as a martial artist, Hwang is popularly known amongst his fans as either the 'Silver Fox' (the name of his character in the movie *The Secret Rivals*), or the 'Lord of the Superkickers', due to the fact that he relies primarily on his legs when fighting.

For a time he instructed the Korean military in unarmed combat, and in self-defence once killed a Vietnamese man who – apparently desiring to see if he was as good at fighting in real life as he was in his films – decided to attack him with a knife.

Officially retiring from acting in the early 1990s

(although he has since made occasional film appearances), Grandmaster Hwang Jang-Lee went on to run a hotel in Seoul, as well as a bodyguard agency.

HYAMS, JOE

Best known for his definitive book *Zen in the Martial Arts*, in which he details his dealings with such masters as **Bruce Lee**, **'Mas' Oyama**, and the 'Father of American Karate' **Ed Parker**.

The chapters of Hyams' book have titles rather than numbers, including 'Empty Your Cup' (in other words: when seeking help or advice, don't try to impress your teacher with what you think you already know), 'Lengthen Your Line' (always focus on improving your knowledge of the martial arts), and 'Active Inactivity' (sometimes it is as important to do nothing as it is something).

In the chapter 'Zen Breathing', Hyams relates how the deep breathing techniques he learnt during a serious of martial arts' classes actually saved his life. On holiday in France with his wife, he contracted Weil's disease – a bacterial infection spread by rats' urine that is potentially fatal. So sick was Hyams that he was both vomiting and voiding blood, and a doctor informed his wife that he was dying.

Only vaguely conscious, Hyams nevertheless knew that unless he fully concentrated on his breathing, the doctor's diagnosis of death would come true. Determinedly, with each breath, Hyams instructed his heart to beat normally and his fever to abate. Finally, as Hyams recovered, he heard the doctor say 'Incredible!'

But in every chapter of this short, well-written book, as Hyams learns a valuable lesson from a particular master, or just through his own, sudden insight, so does the reader.

I

INOSANTO, DAN

One of **Bruce Lee**'s best-known students, Inosanto continues to teach (amongst many other martial arts) Lee's *Jeet Kune Do* philosophy. His Inosanto Academy of Martial Arts, based in California, is also heavily involved in promoting Filipino styles of fighting and training people with various disabilities in the martial arts.

ISHII, KAZUYOSHI

A Japanese *karate* expert (born 1953), Ishii founded the 'K-1' fighting circuit in 1993. K-1 has since become famous worldwide, with its tournaments seeking to determine the best 'stand-up' fighter from such disciplines as *karate*, *tae kwon do*, *savate*, kickboxing and traditional (English) boxing. Ishii's creation made him a wealthy man, though he is, at the time of writing, serving a two-year sentence for tax evasion.

J

JAA, TONY

Born Panom Yeerum in Surin Province, Thailand, on 5 February, 1976, Tony Jaa established himself as a martial arts' film star in *Ong-Bak: Muay Thai Warrior* (2003).

He has trained in numerous martial arts, but somewhat inevitably is best known for his expertise in *Muay Thai*. By all accounts, as a boy aged ten, he threatened his father with suicide should he be disallowed to train in Thailand's best-known fighting art.

A particularly spiritual man, Jaa meditates daily at a Buddhist temple when he is not busy filming. He counts as his pets two elephants named 'Flower' and 'Leaf', and while working as a stunt double for **Sammo Hung** once performed a backwards somersault onto an elephant's back for a drinks' commercial.

JACKS, BRIAN

Britain's youngest ever eighth *dan*, Brian Jacks won a bronze medal in *judō* at Salt Lake City in 1967, and again (aged twenty-six) at the 1972 Munich Olympics. Jacks began training aged ten, and had barely turned fifteen when – at the encouragement of his father, also a *judō* enthusiast – he travelled to Japan to train at the legendary Kodokan (*judō*'s international 'headquarters'). An extremely charismatic character, good-looking and with a beaming smile, Jacks was also ruthlessly efficient when it came to 'studying' a potential opponent, garnering as much information as possible concerning how they moved and what their favourite throw was, down to which hand they favoured using first to grab hold of the other *judoka*'s *gi* jacket. As powerful and as shockingly fast as Jacks' *judō* techniques were, however, he was also not adverse to employing some slightly 'underhand' tactics: on occasion he would eat copious quantities of garlic before a tournament, something guaranteed to make even the hardiest of opponents perform a little below par.

Disillusioned, however, by the poor financial backing that professional *judoka* (at least in Britain) had to endure, Jacks ultimately decided to spread his wings, doing everything from appearing on children's TV shows to delivering motivational speeches to corporate high-flyers. He even had a computer game – *Brian Jacks' Uchi Mata* – named after him, and today remains an irrepressible and truly larger-than-life character.

JUZO, KAEI

During Japan's Tokugawa period, the Shogun ordered that a troublesome *ninja* named Kaei Juzo be captured and killed. Another *ninja* named Tonbe succeeded in completing the first half of this task – only to then realise that Juzo was in fact an old and dear friend.

'I can't kill you,' said Tonbe dejectedly, 'but neither can I return to my master empty-handed.'

'I think I have a plan that will save both our skins,' replied Juzo mysteriously. 'But before you take me to your master, there is something I must find ...'

A short while later, Tonbe brought his prisoner before the Shogun, who immediately ordered that Juzo be put to death.

'Please,' begged the captured *ninja* as he sank to his knees, 'let me take my own life by *seppuku*.'

Seppuku – better known in the West as *hara-kiri* or 'belly cutting' – was an 'honour' traditionally granted to defeated *samurai*. Certainly, *ninja* (who were generally considered to be sneaky and dishonourable) were, if captured, fortunate to receive so much as a quick death – for many suffered the vilest tortures their captor could devise.

The Shogun, however, merely shrugged and allowed

Juzo to take hold of a small dagger which the *ninja* then plunged into his own abdomen. Blood saturated the front of his kimono, and he pitched over onto his side. No one watching had any doubt that that was the end of the troublesome Kaei Juzo.

'Throw his body into the moat,' ordered the Shogun, who then left to attend to more pressing matters.

But the guards who pitched Juzo's body into the water – had they stayed to observe the seemingly deceased *ninja* – would have been amazed by what happened next. For, coming gasping for air to the surface, Juzo then took out the body of a small animal – possibly a rat – that he had found, suffocated and stuffed down the front of his kimono shortly after Tonbe had captured him. As such, it was the rat's blood that the dagger had caused to flow, and not his own. And that very same night, Juzo returned to the Shogun's castle to commit arson, kill some guards, and generally continue to make a nuisance of himself. Only Tonbe, however, knew that he was still alive.

K

KANO, JIGORO

What better title to have than that of 'The Father of Judō'? That is how Jigoro Kano – born in the seaside town of Kikage, near Kobe, in 1860 – is today affectionately known.

Kano's father was both a Shinto priest as well as a government shipping official. His mother died when Kano was nine, and he was sent to a series of exclusive private schools in Tokyo. During his time in education, Kano was repeatedly picked upon by other boys, until in desperation he asked a man called Ryuji Katagiri – whom he knew was familiar with the 'bandit' art of *jujitsu* – to show him some of what he knew.

Katagiri did so, only to then inform Kano that *jujitsu* was not really suitable for someone as puny as himself.

Kano, however, was smitten; he went on to the renowned Tokyo Imperial University where he quickly found a number of different *jujitsu* instructors – commonly osteopaths, who traditionally practised *jujitsu*.

Kano's desire for martial arts' knowledge was something his father had strictly forbidden, believing it would disturb his studies. Kano's father also believed, like many Japanese, that *jujitsu* was for yobs.

But the fact that Kano was prepared to go against his father's wishes (something virtually unheard of at the time) suggests both an uncommon strength of mind and – something almost concealed by his diligent studying – a slightly rebellious character.

Jujitsu training was hard and frequent; sometimes there was not even the luxury of *tatami* mats to land upon, just hard wooden floors. Techniques were shown by the teacher just once; the student had to be sure that he was paying close attention, as he would then have to use the same technique in the ensuing *randori* or 'free practise' sessions.

So determined was Kano to learn – and so hard did he train – that he seems almost to have 'overdosed' on *jujitsu* over the following two years. He would frequently awake screaming the names of various techniques, his quilt soaked in sweat as he kicked it away from his futon.

At the age of twenty-one, Kano was highly skilled in a style of *jujitsu* known as *Tenjin-Shinyo-ryu* ('Divine True Willow School'). He resisted, however, the invitation to graduate from student to teacher, as he considered that he still had a great deal left to learn.

There then came the fateful day when a 200-pound (virtually twice Kano's own weight) student named Kenkichi Fukushima challenged him to a fight. Somewhat inevitably, Kano lost, and, furious, he went away to reflect upon how a small man could actually beat a much larger opponent.

Kano was already obsessed with the idea of making the most efficient use of mental and physical energy. He considered that there was altogether too much wasted effort in the numerous different styles of *jujitsu* – and, besides, which style could be considered 'correct'? Kano had studied *jujitsu* intensively, but he was still often confused about what was and was not correct in terms of technique. And too many teachers were fond of saying that theirs was the only true form.

Also, due to Kano's love affair with the West (he had, through his own endeavour, learnt to speak English fluently by the age of twenty-two), he thought that the martial arts could, like baseball, be a way of uniting people from all backgrounds and classes.

So Kano began adopting (and adapting) techniques that only accorded with his basic philosophy, which he summarised thus:

'To understand what is meant by gentleness or giving way, let us say a man is standing before me whose strength is ten, and that my own strength is but seven. If he pushes me as hard as he can, I am sure to be

pushed back or knocked down, even if I resist with all my might. This is opposing strength with strength.

'*But if, instead of opposing him, I give way to the extent he has pushed, withdrawing my body and maintaining my balance, my opponent will lose his balance. Weakened by his awkward position, he will be unable to use all his strength. It will have fallen to three. Because I retain my balance, my strength remains at seven.*

'*Now I am stronger than my opponent and can defeat him by using only half my strength, keeping the other half available for some other purpose. Even if you are stronger than your opponent, it is better first to give way. By doing so you conserve energy while exhausting your opponent.*'

Kano went back to grapple with Fukushima, who, as before, confidently charged towards him. This time, however, Kano easily beat the much larger man with his devastating *kata guruma* or 'shoulder wheel throw'.

Kano consequently took nine students and established his own *dōjō* or 'training hall' in the Eishoji Buddhist temple. The impact of the students' training, however, quickly caused parts of the temple floor to collapse. Although Kano could frequently be found underneath these sections, armed with a torch and some tools as he sought to repair the damage.

'He may be young, but Mr Kano is really an outstanding man. What a fine person he would be if he would only leave this *judō* alone,' lamented Choshumpo, the head priest, who then insisted that Kano move the *dōjō* to his own home.

So the *dōjō* had to be relocated, and this new *dōjō* was in fact the first incarnation of the world famous *Kodokan*, which remains the headquarters of the *judō* world to this day.

Its fundamental philosophy was that a martial artist had to be able to make mistakes – and yet survive – in order to learn. What was the use if a mistake resulted only in crippling injury or even fatality? Sweat, training, conditioning, and above all else timing, was so much more important than a perfect 'form' in a false environment.

Ultimately Kano took everything that was deemed 'bad' about *jujitsu* – the macho brutality; the excessive risk of serious injury; the unruly, bullying students – out of *judō*, creating a more 'sports-like' martial art that would develop and nurture a young person's mental and spiritual sides – not just their fighting prowess. To put it succinctly, *judō* was deemed to be the physical expression of an ideal society.

Strictly translated, *judō* is 'the gentle way' – and yet, Kano stressed, the use of the word 'gentleness' here was technically incorrect. Better to instead think of the ability to temporarily yield and thus feign defeat, in order that you might win.

Ultimately, it was best to develop *mushin,* or 'no

mind'; to not expend conscious thought on what you are doing; to not trouble yourself with pointless ruminations on 'victory' or 'defeat'. A *Zen*-like frame of mind was the ideal.

Kodokan bylaws were drawn up in 1884, when it was stated that *judō* was intended to promote 'physical culture, mental training, and winning contests'.

A tradition was begun with *kagami biraki* or 'rice-cutting ceremony', when on the second Sunday of every January students ran for miles in freezing conditions, before returning to an equally frigid *dōjō* for a good few hours' worth of training.

In 1886, Kodokan students went up against a powerful *jujitsu* school called *Totsuka ha Yoshin ryu*. Few considered that Kano's lot stood a snowball's chance in hell – and yet they emerged the victors. This firmly put *judō* on the martial arts' map, and started to attract serious and widespread interest in the Kodokan and *judō* in general.

Kano himself was now fast becoming something of a legend; over 160 pounds of well-defined muscle, the strength in his legs in particular widely marvelled over. In fact, Kano was uncharacteristically vain about his legs, on occasion pulling up his trousers to show an unsuspecting visitor his calf muscles.

He was also a workaholic, teaching at a school for the children of Japan's elite, called *Gakushin,* when not at his beloved Kodokan. He would often work late into the night preparing lectures for the following day. When he did relax, it was usually in the rickshaw that took him from one working environment to the other. He was fond of a little *sake*, although he refrained from tobacco all his life.

Kano was married in 1891 to the daughter of the former Ambassador to Korea, and four years later was made headmaster of the Gakushin. This was in spite of his relative youth (he was still only thirty-five). Kano instituted various changes to the school, including making students perform menial tasks such as cleaning so that they might learn humility.

As the nineteenth century dawned, the decline in popularity of *jujitsu* was undoubtedly because of Japan's ever-increasing enthusiasm for *judō*. This was a source of some upset to Kano, given that he had started his martial arts' career with *jujitsu*, and was an expert in several styles before *judō*. It was *jujitsu*, after all, that had allowed Kano to find the way to *judō*.

So, setting aside his basic distrust of *kata* (a series of pre-learned movements), Kano set about doing something that would categorise and preserve at least some of Japan's finest moves and techniques in *budÿ* – 'fighting arts' – which in *samurai* times would have consisted of *jujitsu*, had weapons not been involved.

To this day, a student hoping to become a first *dan* black belt will need to know the *nage no kata*, and many other *kata* as they progress through further *dan* rankings. Kano also asked leading *jujitsu* masters to assist him as he established the training syllabus at the Kodokan. Everyone knew, however, that *judō* was fast replacing *jujitsu* in Japan.

The 1930s saw Japan move ever closer towards war, something that dismayed Kano. He was a pacifist, and thus repelled by the hard-line stance being taken by the Japanese government, who wished to turn his beloved Kodokan into a military academy.

Kano strongly objected to this, and wasn't shy in making his anti-war sentiments known. So much so that, when he apparently died of pneumonia on board a Japanese steamer making its way home from Egypt in May 1938, there was a whisper that he had in fact been murdered by government agents, tired of his vocal opposition.

KIMURA, MASAHIKO

The greatest *judoka* (*judō* practitioner) of all time? Aged eighteen, Masahiko Kimura was the youngest ever *godan* (fifth *dan* black belt), and at the peak of his physical fitness was training nine hours a day and performing 1000 push-ups.

In 1955, aged thirty-eight, Kimura defeated Hélio Gracie (of the legendary Gracie *jujitsu* family) in a fight that caused Gracie to be both choked unconscious (he revived to continue grappling) and have his left elbow broken.

During *randori* (free practise) at the Kodokan – *judō* headquarters – it wasn't uncommon for a number of Kimura's partners to suffer from concussion, Kimura's natural ferocity made even worse by his habit of drinking *sake* before a training session.

Lung cancer eventually killed him at the age of seventy-five, although even on his deathbed he was still performing push-ups.

KOU SZE

Towards the end of China's Qing or Manchu Dynasty (1644–1911), a rather bad-tempered bodyguard named Kou Sze found himself in court accused of killing a man in a fight. Facing the death penalty if found guilty of murder, Kou Sze – a *kung-fu* expert – claimed self-defence, declaring that the dead victim had in fact been part of a gang of four men who had attacked him (Kou Sze) without any provocation whatsoever.

Fortunately for Kou Sze, the judge chose to believe him (the judge's decision no doubt influenced by the large bribe that several of Kou Sze's friends had clubbed together to pay him). However, Kou Sze still received an eight-year sentence for manslaughter, to be served in one of the prison's solitary cells.

Kou Sze resolved to pass his long sentence practising his *kung-fu* – and then, whilst taking a break to look out of his cell window one day, he took notice of the monkeys who were playing in a nearby forest. Soon he began to mimic their actions and movements in his daily training – and by the time he was released from prison, he had perfected the style of *kung-fu* which he called *tai shing* ('great sage' – the name in honour of the monkey king of a popular Chinese folktale). In all, Kou Sze had evolved five different monkey 'forms': the Tall Monkey, the Lost Monkey, the Drunken Monkey, the Stone Monkey, and the Wooden Monkey. And to practise his unique form of *kung-fu* correctly, Kou Sze stressed that it was first necessary to become a monkey mentally – not just imitate one. (Kou Sze failed, however, to elaborate on just how a 'monkey-like' frame of mind might be achieved.)

L

LEBELL, GENE

Described by fans as 'the toughest man alive', Gene LeBell is also much admired by **Chuck Norris,** who, in his book *The Secret Power Within,* describes LeBell as being one of the best martial artists he's ever encountered.

Certainly LeBell's achievements are many: a former American *judō* champion, he also holds ninth *dan* in *jujitsu.* He is equally as famous for his wrestling skills; his heyday being at a time when (as his website describes it) '... wrestling was more about survival than showbusiness ...'.

In late 1963, LeBell accepted a challenge from a little-known boxer who wished to prove that his sport was superior to the oriental martial arts. However, upon arriving for the fight, LeBell was informed that he would actually be facing one Milo Savage – a light–heavyweight who was at the time ranked fifth in the world. Savage was greased from head to foot – to make it next to impossible for LeBell to employ his grappling skills – and also wore a knuckleduster under both gloves. In spite of this, Savage found himself being choked out in the fourth round (he would remain unconscious for a full twenty minutes) and LeBell's popularity increased even further. (The fight is in fact commonly referred to as being 'the day Gene LeBell saved the martial arts', although critics have argued that the aging Savage was in fact hopelessly mis-matched against the much more powerful LeBell.)

At the same time as becoming an internationally famous martial artist, LaBell also became well-known as both a stuntman and author. Once accused by a detrac-tor of having been 'lucky' in all aspects of his approxi-mate fifty-year career, LeBell replied that: '... In life, I find that the harder you work, the luckier you get.'

LEE, BRUCE

No compendium about martial artists would be com-plete without a reference to the man Lee. Student of the legendary Yip Man, martial arts' movie star extraordi-naire, devoted father and husband, Hong Kong's 1958 cha-cha champion – **Bruce Lee** fulfilled many roles before his tragic death aged just thirty-two.

Like Jimi Hendrix in the world of rock music, it is

partly the fact of his early death – with all the resulting myth and speculation that surrounds it – that served to make Lee a legend. And yet he was not superhuman, and neither was he particularly blessed with something that remains beyond the reach of us lesser mortals; he was merely a firm believer in the old maxim: 'No pain no gain', and continually pushed himself towards ever greater goals, both physically and mentally.

Bruce Lee was born in San Francisco's Chinatown in both the year (1940), as well as the hour, of the Dragon. He was only a few months old when he returned with his parents to Kowloon, Hong Kong, where they rented an apartment above a store.

Aged one he made his acting debut in the *Golden Gate Girl*, and throughout his childhood and teenage years would go on to appear in around twenty films. However, by the time he reached his teens, Lee was beginning to run just a little bit wild. In fact, he was fond of strolling around with a steel toilet chain wrapped around his waist, indulging in 'staring competitions' with other young toughs.

The toilet chain proving not wholly effective in several of the ensuing street battles, Lee decided that he needed to improve his 'hand-to-hand' combat skills. So he sought out the legendary Yip Man, desiring to learn *Wing Chun kung-fu*. And learn he did, intensely, day in and day out for the next five years.

By the time he was nearing the end of his teens, Lee's general lawlessness and love of street fighting was beginning to get him in trouble with the authorities. In desperation, his parents packed him off to the place of his birth – San Francisco. During the three-week boat voyage, Lee spent most of his time in First Class teaching the well-heeled passengers how to cha-cha.

Unable to settle in San Francisco, Lee soon moved to Seattle, where he got a job working as a waiter at a Chinese restaurant, living in the room above it. He also began to teach *kung-fu* in local parks and disused basement garages – anywhere, in fact, that afforded him just a little bit of space.

Having found time to earn his high school diploma, Lee was able to enrol at the University of Washington to study Philosophy. Again, (never being one to miss an opportunity) Lee earned a few extra pennies by teaching martial arts to the other students in a building situated close to the university. It was here that trouble came Lee's way: those among the local Chinese community who practised *kung-fu* had long been unhappy about Lee's readiness to teach whoever wanted to learn the martial art, regardless of their race.

One man, Wong Jack Man, came forward with the intention of knocking some sense into Lee: either he stopped teaching Westerners and other, non-Chinese people, or his school would be closed down.

Bruce Lee easily beat the man (at one point Jack Man tried to run away, only to have his exit blocked by a couple of Lee's students), but was troubled by the fact that this victory had taken him three minutes to attain.

Lee realised that he was 'out of shape' (by his own exacting standards, anyway) and that a lot of what he'd learnt in *kung-fu* was ineffective when used in a 'real' situation.

This saw the beginning of what would become **Bruce Lee**'s own style, *Jeet Kune Do* – the 'Way of the Intercepting Fist' – a martial art free of unnecessary frills and what Lee referred to as '... all that classical baloney'.

In 1964 there came a breakthrough for his acting career when he appeared at **Ed Parker**'s martial arts' exhibition in Long Beach, California. There, to an initially dubious and then openly admiring audience, he demonstrated feats of strength such as one-handed and two-fingered push-ups, followed by his famous 'one-inch' punch that propelled an experienced martial artist backwards across the stage. A hair stylist (of all people) for *Batman* witnessed this, and it was something that would lead to Lee's first screen test and resultant casting as 'Kato' in *The Green Hornet.*

The late sixties primarily saw a time of struggle for **Bruce Lee** and his wife, Linda. By now joined by a son, Brandon, they had difficulty making ends meet, although Lee continued to teach and get bit-part work on television.

Later, he would earn approximately $250 an hour teaching Hollywood stars such as Steve McQueen and James Coburn, and become one of the best-known martial artists/movie stars in the world, but for now he had trouble meeting the repayments on his car.

These lean times were followed by something that was potentially far more catastrophic. Performing his usual weight lifting exercises one morning, Lee badly damaged his back. Doctors prescribed several months bed rest, while also informing Lee that he could forget about ever performing martial arts again.

Clawing his way out of a severe depression, Lee passed the time spent recuperating by writing a book concerning his philosophies of his martial art, entitled *The Tao of Jeet Kune Do*. (Published posthumously by his wife Linda.)

Lee defied the doctors' warning by becoming – through sheer hard training and force of mind – an even better martial artist than he'd been before. His back would, however, remain an acute source of pain and discomfort for the rest of his life.

It was while Lee was in Hong Kong, arranging a US visa for his mother, that things really started to happen. First, he was mobbed in the street; little had he known that his role as 'Kato' in *The Green Hornet* had made him famous in this part of the Far East. (It had in fact been renamed *The Kato Show*.) Second, he was offered the lead role in the martial arts' flick *The Big Boss* by film producer Raymond Chow.

This saw the beginning of Bruce Lee's meteoric rise to worldwide fame; *The Big Boss* was followed by *Fist of Fury*, *Way of the Dragon*, *Game of Death* (finished posthumously using a Bruce Lee 'look-a-like'), and the masterful *Enter the Dragon*.

In 1973, however, while resting, Lee suffered a cerebral oedema, or swelling of the brain, and died. Over 25 000 people lined the streets for his funeral in Hong Kong, mourning the untimely death of a genuine Chinese hero.

A much smaller ceremony then took place at Lake View Cemetery in Seattle, with Lee's friend and student, Steve McQueen, being one of his pallbearers.

LEWIS, JOE

Twice voted 'Greatest Fighter in Karate History' by a poll of peers that included Bill 'Superfoot' Wallis, Joe Lewis was also the first World Heavyweight Kickboxing Champion.

While stationed with the US Marine Corps in Okinawa, he earned his *karate* black belt within just seven months and won the US National Championships in weapons, forms and fighting within two years of his first *karate* lesson. As his website is quick to point out, most people are fortunate to have earned their brown belt within a similar time frame.

Today, he is the director of the Joe Lewis Fighting Systems Organisation, and travels around the world attending various martial arts' tournaments and events.

LI, JET

Born in Beijing in 1963, Jet Li (or Li Lian Jie as he was then known) began training early in *wushu*, or the Chi-

nese martial arts. Aged eight he enrolled in the Beijing Amateur Sports School, and by 1974 was performing a *wushu* exhibition for President Richard Nixon on the lawn of the White House. (Apparently, as a 'joke' afterwards, Nixon asked if Li would be interested in becoming his bodyguard in a few years' time. To which Li replied that he was far more interested in protecting Chinamen. According to Li's official website, an embarrassed silence followed this declaration until Henry Kissinger said, 'Heavens, such a young boy and he already speaks like a diplomat!')

Li 'retired' from *wushu* aged seventeen to immediately begin a career in acting. His first movie was entitled *Shaolin Temple* (1982), and brought him immediate success. Some twenty-five more Asian films followed before Li was cast as the villain in *Lethal Weapon 4* (1998), which introduced him to Western audiences and an even greater level of fame.

LI, 'ROSE' SHAO-CHIANG

Born in Beijing around 1914, Shao-Chiang Li was given what was normally a boy's name (which approximately translates as 'continuing strong') by her father, who had seen two other daughters die in infancy. Li's father also enrolled his third daughter in martial arts' training from the age of eight as a way of preserving her health.

Li attended classes in the dramatically named 'Temple of the Fire God', north of the Forbidden City. When she began teaching classes herself, she rejected what she perceived to be the 'macho' side of martial arts (for example, sparring) and instead encouraged her students to focus on the spiritual element.

She became involved in Christian missionary work, moving to America when it became obvious that the communists would shortly be seizing control of China. She later moved to England, where she spent many years teaching until her death in 2001.

LIBERI, FIORE DEI

Medieval master of arms, born in Italy around 1350. He wrote *Flos Duellatorum* ('The Flower of Battle') when aged approximately sixty, an extensively illustrated manuscript composed of short rhyming texts which details comprehensive systems of fighting, both armed (for example, with the poleaxe) and unarmed (there is a section on wrestling), on horseback and on foot.

LONG, KATHY

Boasting such nicknames as 'The Princess of Pain', 'The Countess of KO' and 'The Punisher', Kathy Long is a five-times female World Kickboxing Champion, and holds black belts in several other martial arts' styles, including *aikido* and *kung-fu*.

Beginning her martial arts' training at fifteen, she went on to be named 'Woman of the Year' by the *Black Belt* 'Hall of Fame' in 1991, while *Inside Kung-Fu* magazine declared her 'Female of the Year' in 1992.

She is the author of *NO! NO! NO: A Woman's Guide to Personal Defence and Street Safety*. As an actress, she has appeared in such movies as *Batman Returns* and *Natural Born Killers*. She is also a personal trainer to the rich and famous, including *Batman Returns'* actors Michael Keaton and Michelle Pfeiffer.

LONGHURST, PERCY

Sometime during the start of the twentieth century (probably 1906), expert fighter Percy Longhurst published his training 'manual' *Jiu-jitsu and Other Methods of Self-Defence*. In it he espoused the advantages of becoming proficient in English boxing and wrestling, as well as the Japanese martial art which formed part of his book's title.

However, Longhurst also paid particular attention to two everyday items that could – if wielded correctly – become devastating weapons: namely the humble walking stick (or cane) and umbrella.

A walking stick, wrote Longhurst, was more than capable of '... breaking the wrist of the brawniest ruffian that ever existed'. An umbrella could cause similar injuries; but, cautioned the author, it was never to be used for a direct downward strike, as '... the stick will probably break, and the thick silk will prevent any real damage from being done'. (Longhurst obviously favoured using an umbrella of superior quality.)

The umbrella was rather to be used to jab – into an attacker's eyes, groin (though this was implied rather than written, such a blow no doubt being judged as 'unsporting' even in a life-or-death self-defence situation) and other vulnerable areas, such as the kneecaps.

Sagely, Longhurst advised on how to avoid getting into scrapes with 'homicidal rascals' in the first place by not walking about the streets '... in a half-asleep condition'. (Percy Longhurst was not the only martial artist of his era to concentrate on the self-defence aspects of the walking stick and umbrella; in particular, **Pierre Vigny** and **Edward William Barton-Wright** were two other notable instructors who also recommended their use.)

M

MAN, YIP

Yip Man was born in 1893 to a wealthy merchant family living in Foshan, an old town in southern China at that time famous for its porcelain. He began learning *Wing Chun kung-fu* ('beautiful springtime' is the most common translation, though there are others such as 'forever spring') aged six, learning from a teacher known as 'Money Changer Wan'.

Money Changer got his name through running a coin-changing stall, building up his muscles by carrying around large bags of coins and (presumably) practising his martial arts by beating off the odd would-be mugger or two. So strong was he that it was said he could put a copper coin in the palm of his hand and bend it in two.

Before Money Changer would consent to teaching Yip Man, he first demanded that the young child pay for a series of lessons in advance – and in silver.

So startled was Money Changer when Yip Man managed this seemingly impossible feat that he dragged the boy round by his ear to his parents, convinced that the lad had stolen the money. The parents, however, convinced Money Changer that they'd given their son the money, only too pleased to encourage his fledgling interest.

Yip Man began by learning *Wing Chun*'s 'forms' – solitary exercises that teach the student balance and self-awareness – while also imparting the particular movements necessary for *Wing Chun*.

This style of *kung-fu* was originally formulated by a woman – in fact by a physically slight abbess named **Ng Mui** – and so the emphasis was rather more on timing, strategy, and such things as low kicks to the knees, than on brute force and energy-sapping kicks to the head.

Aged thirteen, Yip Man was making reasonably good progress when Money Changer (who had just a couple of years previously suffered a stroke) was taken seriously ill. Before he died, Money Changer requested that another teacher, Ng Chung-sok, continue training his teenage protégé.

Aged sixteen Yip Man moved to Hong Kong to study English at St Stephen's College. There, his classmates, well aware of his martial arts' prowess and readiness to have a scrap at a moment's notice (usually with Western students, to whom legend informs us he never lost), dared him to mix it with an older man of some fighting repute who lived on a fishing boat anchored in Hong Kong Bay.

This Yip Man did, only to be soundly thrashed in just a couple of moves. The older man then unceremoniously deposited the student into the sea. Crawling back out of the water, Yip Man again went to attack the man, only to meet with exactly the same fate.

And again. And again.

'All right,' said Yip Man finally, soaking wet and beaten black and blue. 'I'll admit that you're too good for me. What's your name?'

'Leung Bik,' replied the older man, fetching his beaten adversary a towel from out of his boat. 'And yours?'

As they forged a slightly friendlier relationship, it was decided that Yip Man should study under Leung Bik. And study he did, diligently, for nigh on eight years.

Finally, Yip Man said farewell to his teacher and returned to Foshan, aged twenty-four. There, he showed the other *kung-fu* students some of what he'd learnt from the fighter in Hong Kong, only to find himself being branded a 'traitor' for the way he'd forsaken the usual ways of training.

'What you've learnt is useless!' the students, and even some of the teachers, mocked him – until Yip Man, his patience exhausted, used his fists and feet to make them retract their comments.

To earn a living Yip Man became a policeman, earning a fair amount of local fame after he tore the gun from the hand of a would-be cop killer. He also taught a number of students – with *Wing Chun* tradition decreeing that he keep his classes small, only teaching those whom he deemed most worthy – right up until the occupation of China by Japan.

Yip Man made himself none too popular with the invading force by refusing to teach their troops *Wing Chun*. Due to this he suffered a certain amount of ill treatment, and was saved from starvation only because his friends gave him illicit gifts of food.

'You've pretty much saved my life,' Yip Man said gratefully to one friend. 'If there's anything I can do for you, you've only to say ...'

'Well,' said the friend thoughtfully. 'There *is* one thing – you know I have a young son who is interested in learning *kung-fu* ...'

So Yip Man was again able to give some lessons: only this time he did so in total secrecy, hiding what he was doing from the Japanese forces by teaching the young boy in a disused cotton mill.

In 1949, repulsed by the rise of communism in China, Yip Man returned to Hong Kong – first staying for a short while in Macao – where in Kowloon he opened a *kung-fu* class specifically for restaurant workers. Money problems (he had for a time something of a gambling addiction) forced Yip Man to change premises several times, and accept those who weren't in the eatery business, but slowly things improved.

From 1954–57 he had one particularly diligent pupil who trained almost daily. This earnest, bespectacled young man was called Lee Siu Lung, later to become known as **Bruce Lee.**

But other students of Yip Man's also went on to become well-known martial artists, and they were all quick to praise their aging teacher for all he'd done for them and for *kung-fu* in general.

Because of this, by the time Yip Man died of throat cancer in 1972 he'd earned himself a certain amount of fame. Through times of trouble and tribulation he'd doggedly continued to teach *Wing Chun kung-fu* – in the process becoming the one man **Bruce Lee** (who was otherwise entirely self-taught) ever accepted as a teacher.

MAO, ANGELA

A martial artist and film actress – born in 1950 and nicknamed 'Lady Whirlwind' by her fans – who appeared in a host of *kung-fu* movies during the 1970s. Originally an actress with the Chinese Opera (whose members are, to this day, referred to as 'Disciples of the Pear Garden' – a reference to the first known acting and musical academy in China during the seventh-century Tang Dynasty), Mao trained in the Korean fighting art of hapkido from an early age.

This stood her in good stead for her first film, *Angry River* (1970). From this she went on take led to leading roles in a number of other movies, including her defining moment in **Bruce Lee**'s *Enter the Dragon*, in which her role as his sister, and her subsequent death at the hands of a bunch of thugs, gives Lee's character a strong motive for revenge.

Capitalising on her success in this movie, her previous films and those made thereafter were released to a Western as well as Asian audience, though by the end of the 1970s she made only a handful more movies, concentrating instead on raising a family.

MATSUMURA, SOKON 'BUSHI'

The *sensei* (teacher) of legendary *karateka* **Gichin Funakoshi**, Master Matsumura was born on the island of Okinawa in 1797. He studied various martial arts in China, and was given the nickname *Bushi* ('Warrior') by the King of Okinawa, for whom Matsumura became Chief Bodyguard. (It seems as though Matsumura's wife was scarcely less formidable than a husband: a respected martial artist herself, she was apparently able to lift – one-handed – huge bags of rice that weighed as much as an average person.)

A tale is still told of how Matsumura went one day to a local engraver's store (why and for what reason does not appear to have been recorded). The engraver himself was a well-built, arrogant *karate* champion, who immediately recognised Matsumura.

The engraver first requested that Matsumura teach him; and then, when this was refused, challenged him to a fight.

'Very well,' said Matsumura amiably. 'Meet me at the graveyard behind Tama Palace at 5 o'clock tomorrow morning.'

'I'll be there,' said the engraver readily, his *kimono* barely containing his bulging muscles.

'One thing I must tell you,' continued Matsumura quietly. 'To fight me is to risk death – I fight all or nothing.'

'You don't scare me,' scoffed the engraver. 'Be worried more about your own death tomorrow morning than mine!'

Matsumura gave a slight shrug.

'I have warned you,' he said, and left the store.

At the appointed time the two men met, the early morning sun still rising. They faced each other, the engraver adopting a formal *karate* stance. Matsumura, however, merely fixed his opponent with an inscrutable gaze that somehow fixed the engraver to the spot. At that moment, somehow, the engraver knew that to attack Matsumura would result only in his own death.

'Well?' said Matsumura, though not arrogantly. 'I am waiting.'

'One ... one moment,' blustered the engraver, attempting to compose himself.

This time, as he prepared to attack, he gave a great *kiai!* This alone had caused many an opponent to crumble in the past – but suddenly a huge bellow from Matsumura himself split the early morning's tranquillity, and the engraver felt his legs give way as he collapsed to the ground.

Matsumura walked over to him, and helped the man up.

'You win,' gasped the engraver. 'Without one blow being struck, you've shown me that to fight you would lead to my death.'

By all accounts the two men then drank tea together; and when they finally parted company, by now firm friends, the engraver was a much wiser and less arrogant man.

MEI, BAK

One of the *Shaolin* Temple's semi-mythical 'Five Elders' (another of whom was Ng Mui), Bak Mei (translated as 'White Eyebrows' – surprisingly enough not his real name) achieved notoriety sometime during the early seventeenth century after he broke the Temple leader's neck in a fight. (He is also meant to have killed several other monks while testing out the new martial art he'd evolved, which he then named after himself.) To top it all, Bak Mei purportedly betrayed the Temple to government forces, who consequently burnt it to the ground.

For these reasons, the 'Bak Mei' system of *kung-fu* (which relies heavily upon close-quarter hand strikes) was traditionally reviled by practitioners of other *wushu* (Chinese martial arts) associated with the *Shaolin* Temple. Bak Mei was represented by the character Pai Mei in Quentin Tarantino's *Kill Bill: Volume 2* (2004).

MUNENORI, YAGYŪ

Japanese swordsman supreme, born in 1571, Munenori taught swordsmanship to the son of the founder of the Tokugawa Shogunate, Ieyasu. So impressed was Ieyasu with Munenori's expertise that he raised his salary to a hefty 10 000 *koku* a year – a *koku* being a measurement of rice that in weight was approximately equivalent to 150 kilograms (and estimated to be enough to feed one man for a year). Thus was Munenori's staple diet assured, at least.

It is reputed that in addition to his superb reactions, Munenori also had an almost superhuman ability to detect approaching danger. This is best illustrated by the story concerning how, one day, an assistant to Munenori decided to sneak up on his master while Munenori was meditating in his garden. The assistant was carrying a sword, however, and had previously harboured some less-than-pleasant thoughts concerning his master.

Barely was the assistant within a few feet of the mediating man when Munenori suddenly jumped to his feet and turned to face his 'adversary', some sixth sense having warned him of impending doom. The assistant grovelled for forgiveness concerning his rank stupidity, and was, by all accounts, forgiven.

MUSASHI

Legendary Japanese swordsman, born in 1584 and given the somewhat lengthy name of Shinmen Musashi no Kami Fujiwara no Genshin. (He is, however, almost universally referred to as just 'Musashi'.) He was raised primarily by his stepmother and older sister, with his father appearing from time to time to teach the boy swordsmanship.

Musashi's first duel was at the tender age of thirteen when he passed a wooden sign that read: 'Whoever wants to challenge me shall be accepted', followed by a name.

Musashi scribbled: 'I will challenge you tomorrow',

adding his name and address. (I guess he took it as read that the sign referred to a duel with swords.)

A duel was arranged the following morning, following the freezing, pre-dawn bath that Musashi was apparently fond of taking. (It's also been claimed that Musashi never washed *at all*, so concerned was he that this might enable an assassin to take him by surprise.)

And so, though barely in his teens, Musashi savoured his first victory, apparently beating his opponent – a *samurai* – to death with a wooden sword.

Another duel followed three years later, and again it brought Musashi some fame locally. Then he fought in the famous Battle of Sekigahara (1600), which paved the way for Tokugawa Ieyasu to become the first Shogun of Japan. Musashi had joined forces with the losing side, however, and was subsequently obliged to hide amongst thousands of corpses for some three days to avoid being captured and killed himself.

A few years later, aged twenty-one, he went to Kyoto, at that time the capital of Japan. He issued a challenge to a powerful warrior named Yoshioka Genzaemon, who at first laughed in the face of this young upstart, until he realised that Musashi wasn't joking. It was Musashi who had the last laugh, though, when Genzaemon lost consciousness during the duel and was thus judged to be the loser. Genzaemon's younger brother attempted to save family honour and face by challenging Musashi, but this time lost not just consciousness but also his life.

Musashi was clearly deadly, and word began to spread ...

A third challenge came from Yoshioka Genzaemon's twelve-year-old son, although this was a blind: instead of a duel, Musashi would instead stumble into an ambush and be cut down by around eighty *samurai*.

Unusually for Musashi, he arrived at the duel early (he was often late, which was construed as being a grave insult to an opponent), when his would-be assassins were still busy concealing themselves. He twigged what was going on, cut down a few of the *samurai* – as well as the unfortunate child who'd issued the third challenge – then took to his heels.

Over the next few years Musashi roamed around Japan, regularly accepting duels that history informs us he never lost. In fact, he got so cocky that – echoing his first duel aged thirteen – he again fought armed only with a crude wooden sword he'd carved himself from an oar. His opponent was so enraged by this slight that he charged at Musashi with his own sword drawn, only to have the wooden sword brought down hard upon his head.

Musashi left him dying on the ground, disdaining the finishing blow that was the norm. (Some sources say that this was because Musashi had to leap into a boat, beating a hasty retreat from his deceased opponent's angry friends.)

Later in his life Musashi appears to have become mildly depressed, turning into something of a recluse and going to live in a cave. But it was in this cave that he wrote his famous *Book of Five Rings,* about philosophy and martial arts in general. He died (probably from stomach cancer) just one week after completing it.

N

NASU NO YOICHI

The *Heike Monogatari* ('The Tale of Heike') details the epic struggle between the Minamoto and Taira clans during Japan's Genpei War (1180–1185). On the side of the Minamoto was the legendary archer Nasu no Yoichi, whose supreme feat of skill is recorded in one section of the *Heike Monogatari*.

The Taira had placed a beautiful golden fan high atop the mast of one of their ships; laughingly, they challenged any of the Minamoto bowmen to try to shoot it off. It seemed an impossible task: not only was the sea rough, causing the ships to bob up and down, but the strong wind would certainly snatch any arrow far from its intended target. But riding his horse out into the surf, Nasu no Yoichi – who at that time was quite possibly still in his teens – put an arrow to his bow and took careful aim. Then, with one shot, he succeeded in knocking the fan off from the mast.

NG MUI

Numerous legends and stories surround this woman, but the following seems to be the most oft told and consistent. During the Ching (or 'Qing') Dynasty, Emperor K'ang-hsi and his Manchurian government felt threatened by the *Shaolin* monastery called Siu Lam of Mount Sung, in Honan province.

K'ang-hsi deemed that the temple had become too powerful through its *kung-fu* training, and sent troops to destroy it. But it has been suggested that it was in fact a treacherous monk named **Bak Mei** who ruined the temple, setting it alight from the inside.

Only a handful of people escaped, including the temple's Abbess Ng Mui, who sought shelter at the White Crane Temple on Mount Tai Leung.

Ng Mui dedicated herself to finding a system of *kung-fu* powerful enough to defeat the Manchurian forces, discarding the old ways of learning as being far too time consuming and impractical.

Why spend years conditioning bones and developing superior muscle strength, she demanded of herself and others, when a bigger, tougher opponent could be defeated with just a finger jab to the eyes, or a lightening quick kick to the groin? Thus Ng Mui developed deadly sounding techniques such as 'flexible reed spine' and 'iron wire continuous return'.

While at the White Crane Temple, perfecting her system, Ng Mui met and befriended a young woman called Yim Wing Chun. Yim (who was still in her teens) owned a bean curd shop with her father, her mother having died while Yim was still a child.

So beautiful was Yim that a local ne'er-do-well had expressed his strong desire to marry her – or, failing that, to take her by force. Yim appealed to Ng Mui to help her, so off went the pair into the mountains where Ng Mui taught the young woman everything she knew.

In something that sounds straight out of an old martial arts' flick, Yim emerged from the mountains to defeat the bully in spectacular style.

In honour of her protégé, Ng Mui named the new, back-to-basics style of fighting she'd managed to perfect *Wing Chun*. And from Miss Wing Chun, we can in fact trace a direct link to **Bruce Lee** – for Yim Wing Chun taught her husband, who in turn taught an opera performer (of all people), and so it continued for a few more generations until a gentleman with the suggestive title of Money Changer Wan found himself instructing a teenage boy called **Yip Man**, who would eventually be the only person to teach Lee – arguably the most famous martial artist ever.

NGUYEN, LOC

Born in 1912 in Vietnam, Nguyen Loc studied martial arts from an early age. This was largely due to the influence of his father, who considered self-defence skills to be necessary in a country that was suffering under French occupation. Nguyen trained long and hard, both at home and abroad, and, aged twenty-six, felt confident enough to introduce to Vietnam the martial art he'd created – which he called *Vovinam Viet Vo Dao*.

Following a demonstration at a theatre in Hanoi, a French Colonel was, somewhat ironically, sufficiently impressed by what he'd seen to award Nguyen a medal. To the delight of his countrymen, however, Nguyen simply stuffed the object in his pocket, for he intended his martial art – which he'd already begun teaching – to serve as a way for Vietnam to be free finally of the French yoke. Consequently, the French authorities attempted to ban it; however, it continued to be taught in secret.

Nguyen was instrumental in the battle for independence which followed the Second World War, and in 1951 founded the Vietnamese Martial Arts Federation. When Vietnam was split into two parts in 1954, he remained in the south, where he died suddenly in 1960.

NICOL, CLIVE WILLIAMS

C.W. Nicol (as he is usually referred to) is a Welshman who has lived in Japan for over forty years. He first went there desiring to study *karate*, and over the following two years changed from being a headstrong, somewhat fiery young man (who even in peaceful Japan managed to get into a couple of punch-ups; once onboard a tram and later while attempting to secure a taxi for himself and his pregnant wife) to eventually become a calm *shodan*. (First-degree black belt.)

In his classic book detailing his experiences – *Moving Zen: One Man's Journey to the Heart of Karate* – he describes how brutally hard training actually taught him the art of tranquillity, and made him realise that the truly strong and powerful are often gentle in character. It is only the weak and the pretenders who have to act 'tough'.

Married to a Japanese woman – and possessing Japanese citizenship – C.W. Nicol has grown famous within his adopted country. This is due to the fact that he has written close to 100 books in Japanese – both fact and fiction – and because of his tireless efforts at preserving Japan's beautiful woodlands from the twin ravages of pollution and construction. He is currently a seventh *dan karateka*.

NORRIS, CHUCK

Real name Carlos Ray Norris, 'Chuck' (born 1940) is
best known to many for his *Missing in Action* movies,
in which he plays hardened war veteran Colonel Brad-
dock who, following the end of the Vietnam War, is on
the hunt for American POWs.

As well as being an actor, however, Norris is also six-
times World Professional Middleweight Karate Champion, retiring undefeated in 1974. This was partly upon
the advice of Steve McQueen, who informed Norris
that he had a promising career in film. In fact, by then
Norris had already appeared in *Way of the Dragon*
(1972) as **Bruce Lee**'s nemesis in the final, epic fight
sequence.

A committed and outspoken Christian (he has publicly denied the theory of evolution, stating that every
creature that has ever lived on earth has been deliberately made by God), Norris is also well known for his
charity work. In particular, he is instrumental in the
'Kick-Start' Foundation, which gives disadvantaged
youngsters the chance of a better life through martial
arts.

In late December 2007, Norris sued the publisher
Penguin for printing a book of Chuck Norris 'facts'.
Intended as humorous satire, the book told how
'Chuck Norris's tears cure cancer. Too bad he never
cries' and, 'Chuck Norris doesn't read books. He stares
them down until he gets the information he wants'.

While Norris declared that he found some of these 'facts' amusing, others were racist, sexist, or generally cast him in a poor light.

O

OHTSUKA, HIRONORI

Founder of the *Wado Ryu* style of *karate*. Ohtsuka's martial arts' training began with *jujitsu* under the tutelage of his great uncle who was, apparently, a samurai warrior. Not until he was thirty (in 1922) was Ohtsuka exposed to *karate*, when he met legendary *Shotokan karate* founder **Gichin Funakoshi**.

So impressed was Funakoshi with Ohtsuka's enthusiasm for all things *karate* that he agreed to show the younger man everything he knew. In time, however, Ohtsuka grew dissatisfied with what he felt was **Funakoshi**'s over-emphasis on *kata*; Ohtsuka felt that *karate* should be a lot 'freer', with less focus on this series of movements and more frequent sparring practise. Butting heads with **Funakoshi** over this (though one presumes not literally), Ohtsuka went on to form his Wado Ryu school of *karate*, which in 1938 was formally recognised within Japan. Ohtsuka died on 19 January, 1982, aged eighty-nine

OSHICHENIKOV, A.

A Russian whose first name appears not to have been recorded, Oshichenikov visited Japan in 1911, where he trained at the Kodokan (*judō* headquarters) for six years.

Returning to Russia, he used what he'd learnt to found a fighting style called 'Sambo' – an acronym of the Russian for 'self-defence without a weapon'– (or 'Sombo', as it's commonly known in the USA), which combined *judō* techniques with a variety of Russian wrestling styles.

Other sources, however, credit Sambo's origins to a number of other men, one of whom, Vasili Oshchepkov, a Red Army Officer, was shot in a gulag during one of Russia's periodic political purges. Another man, Victor Spiridonov, founded a 'softer' style of Sambo called 'Samoz', which has more in common with *aikido* than *judō*.

OYAMA, MASUTATSU 'MAS'

Although he is often mentioned as being one of Japan's finest ever *karateka* (*karate* practitioners), Oyama was in fact born in South Korea in 1923, where he went under the name of Yong-I Choi.

A farm hand instructed Oyama (to avoid confusion, this name will be used throughout) in the martial arts, until Oyama – by now aged fifteen – decided that he wanted to go to Japan to become a fighter pilot.

Taking his new name in honour of a family who briefly looked after him, he soon managed to ruin his dreams of military glory by hitting an officer who sought to bully him.

Lucky to escape without being imprisoned, Oyama decided to devote himself more seriously to the martial arts – and in particular *karate*. He trained long and hard, until one evening he decided to have a little time off and attend a dance at a local hall.

There, he soon found himself obliged to come to the defence of a woman who was being harassed by a drunk.

'Come on,' said Oyama gently. 'I think you've had enough to drink.'

'Mind your own damn business!' spat the drunk, moving to strike Oyama.

Nimbly dodging the blow (Oyama was as fast as he was big), the *karate* expert then dealt the drunk's head a devastating blow with his fist. And although Oyama had in no way meant to kill, the drunk was dead before he hit the ground.

Devastated by the fact that he was now a murderer – and discovering that the dead man had a wife and children – Oyama went to help on the widow's farm.

(Curiously, the widow seems not to have objected to her husband's killer acting as a labourer.)

There he stayed for several months, until the widow apparently forgave him. Purged of his guilt, Oyama returned to *karate* with a vengeance. However, bored with conventional martial arts' training, he decided to test himself on top of a mountain called Mount Minobu in Chiba prefecture. A friend of his delivered some essential supplies once a week, while Oyama awoke at 5 o'clock each morning to train for fifteen hours a day. He used trees to strengthen his arms, fists, legs, feet, and forehead – striking each body part hundreds of times a day – and drove himself beyond the point of exhaustion by repeatedly running up and down the mountainside. Finally, when he felt the need to cool down, Oyama practised his *kata* beneath a freezing waterfall.

Eighteen months passed before Oyama permitted himself a short break, coming down from the mountain to win a number of *karate* tournaments. Then it was back up Mount Minobu, to indulge in another year's gruelling training. Finally, satisfied with what he'd achieved but now seeking a fresh challenge, Oyama decided to pit his strength against a bull. This, he decided, would surely prove to the world that Japanese *karate* was truly a force to be reckoned with.

Oyama ultimately faced over fifty bulls in a bloody showdown between man and beast. In a move which would undoubtedly infuriate animal rights' activists today, Oyama killed three bulls with a straight blow to the head, and deprived most of the others with his legendary 'knife-hand' strike.

One bull, however, succeeded in severely goring the skilled *karateka*. Oyama was not expected to survive his injuries, although after a lengthy period spent recuperating he was once again fighting fit.

Oyama subsequently decided to start his own *karate* school, where brutal 'knock-down' sparring and runs bare-chested in the snow were standard training. Anyone who failed to show what Oyama considered to be sufficient 'spirit' soon found themselves out on their ear.

After a long battle against lung cancer, Oyama (a non-smoker) passed away on 26 April, 1994, aged seventy-one.

P

PANICKER, SIMHALAN MADHAVA

Born in 1930, Simhalan Madhava Panicker left home aged just eight to travel around India pursuing his combined dream of becoming an expert martial artist and actor. He achieved both goals, appearing in many films and eventually (after years of intensive training) being recognised as a world authority on *Varma Kalai*.

Varma Kalai is a division of the ancient South Indian martial art *Kalaripayattu* (which it is claimed Bodhidharma practised), which teaches its practitioners to attack specific, secret parts of the body, believed to be the junctions of blood vessels and certain nerve nodes. (Indeed, *Varma Kalai* can be translated as 'the art of certain points'.) When such points are struck, anything from intense pain to instantaneous death can be caused, depending on the attacker's wishes. (*Varma*

Kalai practitioners are, however, taught to use the least necessary force to overcome their opponent. Ironically, *Varma Kalai* began life many hundreds of years ago as a healing – rather than a martial – art.)

Panicker accepted very few students during his lifetime, but all those who trained under him became expert martial artists themselves. Panicker passed away in March 2004, while his daughter, Jasmine Simhalan (born 1970) is herself a famous martial artist and dancer.

PARKER, EDMUND KEALOHA

Parker was the founder of 'American Kenpo', a comprehensive self-defence system that borrowed heavily from a number of different martial arts, but was associated by most of its practitioners (including Elvis Presley, for whom Parker acted for a time as bodyguard) with Japanese *karate*. Thus Ed Parker became known as 'Mr Karate', or 'The Founder of American Karate'.

In 1990, at the age of just fifty-nine Ed Parker died of a heart attack.

PICHAI, PHRAYA

Born in 1741, Phraya Pichai was, from early childhood, fond of practising *Muay Thai* kickboxing, to the point that when his parents forbade him from doing so, he continued to train in secret.

When he was aged around twenty, Pichai went to a

festival that was being held in a town called Tak. There was a ring set up, inside of which was a famous fighter named Arjan Nai Hao, whom no one had yet dared challenge.

'I'll fight him!' called out Pichai from the crowd.

Up he went into the ring, where an overconfident Hao charged towards him. In spectacular fashion, and much to the watching crowd's amazement, Pichai soon beat him.

Also watching that day was Phraya Taksin, the future king of Siam (present-day Thailand) – for the country was at that time under Burmese occupation – who was quick to make Pichai his personal bodyguard.

With the Burmese forces engaged in fighting the Chinese, General Taksin (as he was then known) soon succeeded in raising an army of which Pichai was made Commander-in-Chief.

Pichai easily translated his *Muay Thai* skills onto the battlefield, with the result that the Burmese were driven out of Siam and General Taksin made king.

It was tradition that when the king died his bodyguards and most loyal servants were executed. However, his successor, King Rama, stated that in Pichai's case an exception could be made. So invaluable had he been in securing his country's freedom from an occupying force, that his life would be spared.

'That means nothing to me,' said Pichai sadly. 'My king is dead – please, kill me too.'

Perplexed, King Rama nevertheless granted the

41-year-old fighter his wish. In 1969 a bronze statue was made to honour him, the inscription: *In Memory and Loving Honour for the Pride of Our Nation.*

POLLY, MATTHEW

The author of *American Shaolin* (2007), and a self-declared '... skinny little 98-pound weakling' whose desire to learn authentic *kung-fu* caused him to travel from his native Kansas to China's legendary *Shaolin* Temple.

Polly is an engaging and often humorous author who writes candidly about his struggle to prove to himself that he is a 'man' through learning *kung-fu*. At one stage, suffering from acute nervous diarrhoea shortly before competing in a tournament fight, he nevertheless ultimately finds the strength through his experiences to face down several Triad (the Chinese 'mafia') members who have been harassing a friend of his.

Polly attempts to develop an 'iron arm' – that is, one which will have incredible destructive power – while his description of the type of 'training' necessary to give oneself an 'iron crotch' (backed up with photos) will leave most male readers wincing.

POWELL, MOSES

Born 13 January, 1941 in Norfolk, Virginia, Doctor Moses Powell undertook years of training in various styles of martial arts – including *karate* and *jujitsu* – before founding his own style called 'Sanuces Ryu Jujitsu'.

He created the word '*Sanuces*', claiming that it was similar in meaning to 'simplicity' or 'survival'. It is like water, something that can be either a trickle or a flood, life or death.

Sanuces Ryu *jujitsu* was (and still is) designed specifically 'for the street', containing lots of no-nonsense striking and pressure point techniques. Doctor Powell taught his style to both the FBI and the CIA, and had instructed thousands of students by the time of his death on 22 January, 2005.

PRAPRADANG, POL

Born in 1921, Prapradang was a *Muay Thai* boxer who became known as the 'Wild Boar' due to his fighting skill and general ferocity. He willingly fought outside of his own weight division – against much larger and heavier men – and in approximately 350 matches was never knocked out nor even given the count. A character perpetually bursting with energy, Prapradang was almost as well known for the dance called *Hanuman Tob Yoong* ('The Monkey God Slapping the Mosquito') which he performed before each match, as he was for his fighting.

Only when he considered himself too old to fight did

he stop, concentrating instead on his career as a police officer. (Which, presumably, still saw him getting involved in the odd scrap.) He died in 1977, aged fifty-six.

R

RHEE, JHOON GOO

Very few martial artists can claim to have taught **Bruce Lee** anything, yet it was, by all accounts, the 'Father of American Tae kwon do', Jhoon Rhee, who gave the up-and-coming film superstar a few tips on his kicking techniques. (Muhammad Ali was also more than happy to have Rhee advise him on how best to punch.)

Seventy-six at the time of writing, Rhee has a daily exercise regime that would cause most men half his age to collapse – at least 1000 push ups, with a similar number of sit ups. (He performs these exercises even when travelling on a plane, cabin crew permitting.) A lifelong teetotaller and non-smoker, he eschews meat in favour of a diet which is rich in water, fish and vegetables.

Coming from Korea to America in the 1950s with barely $50 to his name (and apparently because he was captivated by blonde American female film stars), Rhee soon succeeded in establishing a string of training halls in the Washington area – the number of which has only increased over time. He also opened several venues in the former Soviet Union following the end of the Cold War.

And the motivation for Rhee to dedicate his life to the martial arts? Well, at the age of six he was slapped by a girl while they were at school. Seeking sympathy, Rhee returned home crying to his mother – who merely slapped him harder and told him to learn to defend himself. Advice which, it's quite clear, Rhee took to heart.

ROTHROCK, CYNTHIA

American martial artist and film star, Cynthia Rothrock (born 1957) is the holder of five black belts in Chinese and Korean martial arts. She is also an expert user of various types of weaponry, including the legendary Chinese 'Iron Fan'.

Rothrock's first exposure on the big screen came in the form of a Kentucky Fried Chicken commercial. Soon, however, her first full-length film, *Yes Madam!*, proved to be a smash-hit in Hong Kong – something that led Rothrock to spend much of the following half decade there, making films for a predominantly Asian audience.

The *China O'Brien* movies (*China O'Brien* and *China O'Brien 2*) represented an attempt at breaking Rothrock into the United States' movie market. Although not initially as successful as her previous films, they soon garnered a cult following within the Western, video-watching world, and led to her making more films in various exotic climes.

S

SASUKE, SARUTOBI

In finest *ninja* tradition, no one seems certain whether or not Sasuke Sarutobi actually existed. Often mentioned in the stories told to children in the early twentieth century, he remains to this day something of a staple in *manga* (Japanese for 'comic').

Sarutobi means 'monkey jump', and legend informs us that the young Sasuke was in fact raised by monkeys, thus inheriting their agility and ability to swing from tree to tree. Pity the poor swordsman who later had to face the *ninja* Sasuke had become – for as he ducked and dived here, there and everywhere, it proved quite impossible to kill or injure him.

Sasuke was (in fact, or maybe just in fiction) an associate of Kirigakure Saizÿ, who was the smoother, more handsome and more debonair of the pair.

Kirigakure, incidentally, means 'hidden in fog'; clearly, with their respective powers, he and Sarutobi were a formidable couple of fighters.

(In his excellent book *Ninjutsu: The Art of Invisibility*, **Donn F. Draeger** describes how Sarutobi – assuming that he actually existed – met his end. Whilst on one of his many missions, he was spotted by some guards and chased into a bear trap. Valiant to the end, Sarutobi amputated his own foot in a bid to make good his escape – but to no avail. Realising that the guards were almost upon him, the maimed *ninja* chose to fall upon his sword rather than face capture.)

SDE-OR, IMRICH

The founder of the much-lauded *Krav Maga* fighting system, Imrich Sde-Or was born in Budapest in 1910. He grew up in Slovakia, his father – a man named Samuel Lichtenfeld – a wrestler and weight lifter in a travelling circus. Lichtenfeld, along with some other members of the circus, taught the young Imrich (or 'Imi', as he was generally known) a variety of wrestling and fighting styles.

Imrich trained so diligently that in 1928 he won the Slovakian Youth Wrestling Championships, triumphing just one year later in the adult division too.

During the mid 1930s, some dark clouds began to gather over Slovakia. Fascist groups appeared, determined to intimidate and harm the country's Jewish community. Imi Sde-Or led a group that fought back, giving the fascists a taste of their own medicine using their combined skills in unarmed combat.

Well aware that his life was in continual danger, however, Sde-Or was at last persuaded, aged thirty to board a ship that was carrying a mass of refugees from central Europe to Palestine.

From 1944, he started training anyone who wanted to learn various fighting techniques; and in 1948, when the State of Israel was founded, he was appointed Chief Instructor of Krav Maga.

Sde-Or continually sought to refine his martial art, stripping everything back to the bare basics that a person (who may not have any particular physical ability) requires to deal with an armed or unarmed encounter.

Sde-Or passed away on 9 January, 1998, having seen his fighting art becoming popular right across the globe for its no-nonsense style and simple, effective techniques.

SEAGAL, STEVEN

Born in 1951, the 6-foot 4-inch Steven Seagal is considered to be as unflappable in real life as he is in his action movies, which include *Marked for Death* and *Executive Decision*. A seventh *dan aikido* expert,

Seagal moved to Japan soon after graduating from high school in California, and for a time ran his own *dōjō* in Osaka. He then returned to America to concentrate on establishing a movie career. (He made his acting debut in *Above the Law*, 1988.)

Steven Seagal is also an accomplished blues guitarist, and has released a number of albums that feature contributions from such musicians as B.B. King and Stevie Wonder. A committed Buddhist, he has been 'recognised' by a Tibetan Lama as being the reincarnation of a seventeenth-century monk named Chungdrag Dorje. He actively supports a number of charities, including the African AIDS project Save a Million Lives.

SHAN, LIU FENG

Also often called Liu Cai Chen, Feng Shan was a famous *wushu* practitioner who was born in the Ningchin district of Hebei in 1852.

Almost as soon as he was able to walk, his parents ensured that he was trained in *wushu*. Upon their death (which occurred when Feng Shan was barely in his teens) he left for Beijing, hoping to find a teacher there who could further instruct him.

Feng Shan entered a city that was markedly different to the staid rural life he'd left behind. During the late 1900s Beijing was a veritable melting pot of cultures, where it was not uncommon to find great palaces adorned with golden statues of dragons situated next to ornate mosques. Travelling swordsmen gave way to fleets of camels laden down with anything from packages of spices to exotic rugs, all imported from far-flung countries; no wonder that the young Feng Shan stared with wondrous eyes at all he surveyed.

For several years, however, Feng Shan found life in the city to be anything but easy. He took on a number of jobs, none of which paid him anything more than the bare minimum he needed to survive. At last, however, he succeeded in finding a *wushu* teacher of considerable repute.

Liu De Kuan (the teacher) made a handsome living hiring out guards to protect the homes and possessions of the wealthy. (Given that China was at this time infested with bandits, such protection was something of a necessity.) At first De Kuan refused to accept Feng Shan as a student, until the teenager finally impressed him with both his determination as well as his existing *wushu* ability.

'Okay,' said De Kuan at last, 'I'll show you what you want to know. But, believe me, I'm a strict man. You'd better do just as I say, without question or hesitation.'

De Kuan wasn't lying; Feng Shan found himself having to train harder and longer than he ever had before. Eventually both student and teacher left Beijing, hiring themselves out as travelling guards. Feng Shan was by now around thirty years old, and known as 'The Big Spear' due to his awesome ability with this weapon.

Finally, De Kuan passed away, and due to their combined business interests Feng Shan returned to Beijing a wealthy man.

He continued to train in *wushu* as all around him in the city the 'Society of Harmonious Fists' (or 'boxer's, as they were known in the West) rioted, attacking anything and anyone not of Chinese descent. It was, to put it mildly, a particularly fractious and violent time.

In 1912 Feng Shan helped found the 'Beijing Research Institute of Physical Education', something which accorded with Feng Shan's primary goal in life – to promote *wushu* as a way of obtaining physical and mental health for the Chinese people.

Certainly it seems to have worked for Feng Shan, who, well into his eighties, remained perfectly healthy. And until the day he died he preached that just three things were essential for the successful cultivation of *wushu*: practise, time, and insight.

SHIGENOBU, HAYASHIZAKI JINSUKE

Shigenobu was the founding father of modern-day *Iaido* – the art of drawing one's sword (*katana,* in Japanese) and of attacking one's enemy in one continuous movement.

Born into a *samurai* family sometime around 1546, Shigenobu's father was killed in a duel when his son was aged about twenty-five. Obsessed with the idea of revenge, Shigenobu went to a *Shinto* shrine where he stayed for 100 days in concentrated prayer and study, practising how he might draw his sword and kill his opponent in one swift, sure, and utterly deadly movement.

Naturally, legend tells of how, once those 100 days were up, Shigenobu found and killed his father's assassin pretty damn quickly. He then went on to establish his own *Iaido* school. (*Iaido* practitioners today can expect to start learning with a *bokken*, or 'wooden sword'. Only those who have become masters of this martial art are permitted to train using a real weapon.)

SING, PAK

A legendary 'iron palm' master – that is, someone whose hands were so hardened by martial arts' training that he was able to 'slap' assorted bricks and rocks in half.

Indeed, so expert was Pak Sing that he could slap a stack of bricks and only break one perhaps four or five down – the same brick he'd said he'd break *before* performing the task.

SMITH, ROBERT W.

A martial artist and historian who – along with such men as **Donald 'Donn' Frederick Draeger** and **Jon**

Bluming – did much to introduce Asian fighting arts to the West.

A former US Marine, born in 1926, Smith was already an accomplished boxer and wrestler by the time he was posted to Taiwan as a CIA operative.

While in Taiwan he became *tai chi chuan* master **Cheng Man-ch'ng**'s first non-Chinese student. This caused Smith's interest in Chinese and other Eastern martial arts to develop, and so he set about recording what he saw and learnt in a series of well-written books and articles. He published his memoirs, *Martial Musings*, in 1999.

SO, DOSHIN

Born in 1911, Doshin So was the founder of the martial art (and, in Japan, registered religion) *Shorinji Kempo*, or 'Shaolin Temple Fist Method'. So spent much of his early life in China, where he served as a secret agent for Japan's ultra-nationalistic Black Dragon Society, while also making an extensive study of martial arts. Finally, he was made 21st Master of the Northern Shorinji Giwamonken School at a ceremony held at the fabled *Shaolin* Temple.

Upon returning to Japan in 1946, So was dismayed at his country's ruin following the end of the Second World War. He therefore constructed a small *dōjō* (in conditions of some secrecy, for the American occupational forces had at that time banned the martial arts within Japan) where his students could focus on improving their physical, mental and spiritual (So was a committed Buddhist) health.

Obsessed with improving society through his teachings, So's motto became: *Hito! Hito! Hito! Subete wa hito no shitsu ni aru!* ('The person! The person! The person! Everything depends upon the quality of the person!')

Doshin So – or *Kaiso* ('founder') as he had by now become known – died in 1980, but *Shorinji Kempo* continues to flourish around the world.

SUKUNE, NOMI NO

The *Nihon Shoki* ('Chronicles of Japan'), finished in 720, records a fight-to-the-death that took place in front of the Emperor Suinin around 23 BC.

Taima no Kuyehaya was one of the fighters; a huge, arrogant man fond of boasting about his ability to break the horns off cattle and straighten out iron hooks.

'If only I could meet another man of equal strength and fighting ability, how happy I would be,' he sighed, little suspecting that his wish was soon to be granted. Though whether he was happy or not at the moment of death is another matter.

At the Emperor's specific request, a man called Nomi

no Sukune was found to challenge Kuyehaya. Little background information surrounds Sukune, except for the fact that he was considered 'valiant', but in any case Sukune quickly succeeded in kicking Kuyehaya to death, with the Emperor enthusiastically watching on.

By way of reward, all of the deceased man's land and property was confiscated and given to the fight's victor, who then disappeared back into history.

Some view this fight as being the first recorded account of unarmed combat, while others go further, classing Taima no Kuyehaya (that great bull of a man) as a *rikishi,* or *sumo* wrestler, and Nomi no Sukune (the kicker) as being the practitioner of something broadly similar to *jujitsu.*

Thus could that fight of so many centuries before have been the very first 'mixed martial art' tournament.

SUN, LU-T'ANG

Born in 1861, when just a young boy Sun Lu-t'ang was obliged to start working for a cruel landowner after his father, a farmer, died. Physically weak and malnourished, Sun endured many beatings at the hands of the landowner and his son, and became so distressed that he attempted suicide.

Finally, he began to study *tai chi chuan* under a local teacher; he also built up his strength by finding and eating wild vegetables and herbs. Sun proved a quick learner, but lost his job the day he avenged – with his fists and his feet – the ill-treatment he'd previously been forced to endure.

However, he subsequently found employment with his uncle and, whilst studying under several other martial arts' teachers, began to develop his own style of *tai chi chuan*. (Somewhat obviously, this style became known as 'Sun'.)

At the age of nearly sixty he instructed the Chinese army in *wushu* (martial arts), and was given such nicknames as 'First Hand under the Sky' and 'Smarter than an Active Monkey'. (Both these nicknames were, presumably, intended to be complimentary.) He also published several books relating to *wushu*, and in 1933 died peacefully – apparently in the same room in which he was born – aged seventy-two.

T

TALHOFFER, HANS

This fifteenth-century fencing master from southern Germany wrote a number of illustrated accounts concerning the use of the sword, axe, club, dagger, how to fight on horseback and how to wrestle, and also the best way for a husband and wife to have a scrap.

As he wrote beside one illustration of his 'Fight between man and wife': 'This one shows him pulling her to him and throwing her under himself and he means to throttle her' (*sic*).

It wasn't all one-sided, though; the wife could fight back. As captions another illustration: 'She strikes the veil around his throat and means to choke him'.

Thus is everyone happy.

TEIJUN, PRINCE

The sixth son of Emperor Seiwa (850–880 AD) who founded *daito aikijutsu* – the 'father' of present-day *aikido*. And that, unfortunately, is about as much as we know about young Prince Teijun.

TELL, WILLIAM

Although, as with **Robin Hood**, there exists considerable doubt over whether William Tell actually existed, he surely deserves a mention here due to his fabled skill with the crossbow. In the early fourteenth century (so the legend goes), Tell refused to bow before a pole on top of which an Austrian governor named Gessler had placed his hat. (At that time, the Austrians had occupied Tell's region of Canton of Uri, in Central Switzerland.) Gessler, who seems to have been a particularly nasty individual, was about to have Tell executed for his defiance when he suddenly had another idea.

'Okay, smart-guy,' he said. 'If you're so good with a crossbow, like they say, shoot an apple off the top of your son's head at eighty paces.'

'No way,' replied Tell.

Gessler merely shrugged.

'In that case, I'll have you killed right now,' he declared.

Quickly, Tell decided that he would be able to fulfil

Gessler's challenge without harming his young son. But after the apple had been split, Gessler demanded to know why Tell had had another bolt ready.

'That one was for you, in case you hurt my boy,' answered Tell readily.

Enraged, Gessler ordered that Tell be bound and taken by boat across a lake to the governor's castle. But when a storm blew up, Tell was able to make good his escape and return to dry land. Getting his hands on a crossbow, he then sought out and killed Gessler, sparking a rebellion against the hated Austrians that led to the formation of the Swiss Confederation.

(Some years later, Tell is reported as having met his end whilst trying to save a child from drowning in a river. The Altdorf or Tell Monument – a bronze statue of William Tell and his son, erected in 1895 and situated in the market place of Altdorf, Canton of Uri – marks the spot where Tell was supposed to have performed his feat of marksmanship all those years before.)

THOMPSON, GEOFF

An English 'reality' martial artist and BAFTA award-winning writer, born in 1960, who conquered a fear of violent confrontation by working as a doorman on one of Coventry's roughest nightclubs during the 1980s.

During his time at 'Busters' (the name of the club,

though by no means the only establishment where he was employed), Geoff Thompson stood shoulder-to-shoulder with men who'd never done a day's martial arts' training in their lives – but who still had much they could teach him. Thus in real-life, flesh-and-blood battles, Thompson quickly learnt that much of what is learnt in the *dōjō* is, at best, ineffective in real life.

Thompson has taken his experiences 'on the door' and turned them into one of the most realistic types of training it is possible to receive. In his classes, videos and seminars, expect swearing, 'role-play' (aggressor/victim) and lots of advice on how to conquer man's oldest and perhaps worst enemy – his own fear.

Thompson's experiences are well recounted in his autobiography, *Watch My Back*. He has also published many other books, a number of which – based upon Thompson's own battles with depression, agoraphobia and anxiety – have a distinct 'how to help yourself' theme. An expert in, amongst other disciplines, *karate*, *kung-fu* and *judō* (he has been instructed in the latter by former World Champion **Neil Adams**), he has been joint Chief Instructor of the British Combat Association with **Peter Consterdine** since 1993.

TIGER KING, THE

Long ago, Phra Chao Sri Sanpetch, the 29th king of Krung Sri Ayutthaya, was overseeing a 'golden age' in his kingdom where every soldier was trained in *Muay Thai* kickboxing.

The king himself was considered very good at the martial art, and trained daily. There was, however, just one problem – hardly any man could be found to train with him, and those that did ensured that they always lost a match without landing even one blow.

'Why is this?' pondered the king one day, somewhat vexed at his lack of sparring partners.

A courtier delicately cleared his throat.

'Perhaps, your Majesty,' suggested the courtier, 'it's because just to touch you is to be put instantly to death.'

The king nodded solemnly.

'It seems to me that you speak the truth,' he agreed. 'What I must do is to go somewhere nobody knows me, and, once there, seek out a challenge from a champion fighter.'

Soon enough, the king heard of a fayre that was taking place at a temple some distance away. So off he went with a few trusted followers, donning a disguise just in case. (It is not said what this disguise consisted of, though presumably it wasn't a false nose and a pair of spectacles.)

Reaching the temple, the king sought out the promoter who was arranging that day's entertainment – *Muay Thai* kickboxing – and informed the man that he'd gladly be put against any fighter, any size.

The king won his first fight, and then his next – and, it is claimed, lived until his dying day fighting regularly but never once losing.

TIT, KIU SAAM

One of the 'Ten Tigers of Canton' (along with **Wong Yan Lam**), Tit Kiu Saam was born in 1815 and from a young age studied martial arts under the intriguingly-named 'Golden Hook'. Apparently he was also particularly partial to the company of Buddhist monks, whose presence he is said to have found both intellectually stimulating and extremely restful.

Unfortunately he became hopelessly addicted to opium – and although he continued to train hard in the martial arts, managing to reach an extremely high level, his habit eventually killed him.

TOTSUKA, JIRO

Jiro Totsuka was aged just five when his father, a *ninja*, was captured by a *daimyō* (feudal lord) named Kuwana. Totsuka senior had been on a mission to kill Kuwana; but the *daimyō* had his opulent residence fitted with an array of anti-*ninja* devices, from well-trained guard dogs to deep pits that were concealed in corridors beneath collapsible flooring. It was the second device that had caused Totsuka senior's capture.

A *ninja* who'd been caught invariably attempted to commit suicide, often by biting off his own tongue. This was due partly to the sheer indignity of having failed in their mission, but also because they were rarely granted a quick death by their captor.

Totsuka's own demise illustrates this point succinctly – for he was skinned alive. Upon learning of his father's bloody death, Jiro swore revenge. One way or another, he would kill Kuwana. But how to succeed where his own father had failed?

Jiro thought long and hard, and then succeeded in befriending Kuwana's young son, who was of a similar age to himself. Jiro frequently found himself being invited to play within Kuwana's residence, where the *daimyō*'s son proudly pointed out the many traps designed to ensnare an unwitting *ninja*. He even gleefully recounted the story of Totsuka's capture, quite unaware that he was doing so to the deceased *ninja*'s son. Kuwana himself felt an affection for his son's new friend, so much so that, on occasion, Jiro found himself being patted on the head by his father's murderer.

After a time, Jiro had a complete map of the building, with all its assortment of *ninja*-defeating devices, stored within his nimble young mind. Then, as the second anniversary of his father's death approached, Jiro decided to act.

So it was that one day, Kuwana's son suddenly discovered that his playmate was no longer by his side. He could only decide that Jiro had got bored and left the building to return home. Jiro had, however, done nothing of the sort. He had in fact concealed himself above the ceiling in Kuwana's splendid bedroom, where he now waited patiently for the evening so that he might then descend.

It was late when the *daimyō* – who slept alone – decided to retire for the night. Soon, his loud snores informed Jiro that he'd fallen soundly asleep. Quickly, the young lad made a small hole in the ceiling, directly above where he estimated Kuwana's head to be. (It should be said here that Kuwana's bedroom ceiling was beautifully decorated, with Kuwana demanding that his bed always be in exactly the same position beneath it. This would prove to be a fatal error – other *daimyō* in fear of *ninja* attacks rarely slept in the same room for more than two consecutive nights.)

Jiro had guessed correctly – staring directly down, he could just about see that the *daimyō*'s mouth was wide open. This suited Jiro perfectly: first, he lowered down a length of string, so that its end dangled just above Kuwana's lips. Then, from a vial that Jiro always carried on his person, he placed a drop of deadly poison onto his end of the string. Down it slid, taking barely half a minute before it fell inside Kuwana's mouth. And as its bitter taste briefly awoke the *daimyō* – who knew in that instant that he would soon be sleeping the deepest sleep of all – Jiro silently made his way across the ceiling beams until he was above another, empty room, into which he could descend and from there make his escape.

At the age of seven, Jiro Totsuka had succeeded in avenging his father.

TUAH, HANG

Still famous throughout Malaysia for his courage and fighting skill, Hang Tuah lived during the fifteenth century. Instructed from a young age in *silat* – the umbrella term given to both armed and unarmed Malay martial arts – he was little more than a youth when he and four friends allegedly saved a high-ranking government official from some marauding pirates. This led to Tuah becoming a bodyguard to the sultan, with Tuah willingly fighting anyone who sought to 'make their name' by taking him on.

By all accounts, Tuah was utterly devoted to his master. Indeed, after failing to secure the sultan a young and particularly beautiful princess, as he'd been instructed (it didn't help that the princess, as part of her dowry, demanded such hard-to-get items as a colossal bridge made of solid gold and seven trays of mosquito livers), so dismayed was Tuah that it's rumoured he simply vanished into thin air.

TWIGGER, ROBERT

In *Angry White Pyjamas* (1997), this *aikido* practitioner details the intensive year he spent earning his black belt with the Tokyo riot police. (Given the general absence of riots within Tokyo, and indeed Japan as a whole, I guess the 'riot police' have to be kept busy somehow.)

Twigger delights in detailing every sweat-stained, panting, bone-crushing and vomit-inducing moment of his training. This undoubtedly helps to sell the book, although he has been accused of somewhat over-dramatising what actually occurred. (To which he would as likely as not reply: 'Okay, *you* go and do it then.)

Twigger's account details all the highs and lows (with there being many more lows than highs) of intensive martial arts' training and, unlike many other such books, fails to include any reflections on the paths of spirituality and *Zen* learned in the *dōjō*. On the contrary, once the course has concluded, Twigger writes how his frequent bursts of aggression – fine-tuned in the *dōjō* – lead him to 'stare down' anyone who catches his eye in the street.

U

UESHIBA, MORIHEI

The founder of modern-day *aikido*, Ueshiba (1883–1969) was frequently sickly as a child, which caused him to stay indoors and develop his mother's love for poetry and literature. It was only when he witnessed a gang of thugs inflict a violent assault upon his father that Ueshiba realised the benefits of physical activity – in this instance, the martial arts.

During the Russo–Japanese war (1904–1905) Ueshiba attempted to join the army, but was rejected on account of his height. (He stood barely five feet tall.) So dejected was Ueshiba by this that he went into a forest and hung from the branch of a tree in an attempt to make himself taller. By all accounts he was successful – in any case, the army accepted him when he went and applied for a second time.

The freezing climate of northern Manchuria took a severe toll upon Ueshiba's health, and following the end of the war he returned to his parents' farm to recuperate. There he found a *jujitsu* instructor, and through training recovered his previous vigour and stamina.

He then moved with his wife to Hokkaido, where he continued to train. So diligent was Ueshiba in his efforts that it's said he possessed enormous strength in his arms. However, bad news came from his parents' farm: his father was seriously ill, and he died before Ueshiba could complete the return journey home.

In the midst of his grief, Ueshiba – who was something of a spiritual man – did some serious thinking about the martial arts and life in general. In particular, he realised that *budÿ* ('the warrior's way') was not actually about fighting – but more about harmony and love.

In other words, meet violence with violence and chaos and discord are the only things that can result; but counter an attack with a move that absorbs such violence, thus neutralising its negative energy, and you will always emerge the victor.

Thus *aikido* began to emerge; as something that can be studied both as a general way of life, as well as a martial art.

UKIFUNE, JINNAI

As well as being an expert *ninja*, Ukifune was also a dwarf who stood barely three feet tall. He was employed by the sixteenth-century Japanese *daimyō* (feudal lord) Oda Nobunaga – popularly known as the 'Demon King'. Nobunaga was locked in conflict with Uesugi Kenshin, another *daimyō* (there were, at that time, many in Japan), with both men having aspirations to rule the entire country.

Nobunaga had previously used the *ninjas* under his command to try to assassinate Kenshin, but all attempts had been in vain. But then Nobunaga had a brainwave; summoning the dwarf Ukifune, the Demon King ordered the diminutive *ninja* to spend the next few days sleeping in a large earthenware jar. Ukifune asked no questions, but did as instructed. Only after he'd fulfilled this curious request was he told exactly what he needed to do next.

Some days or weeks later, Uesugi Kenshin was within his opulent residence when he realised that he needed to answer a call of nature. So he went to the lavatory, hoisted up his *kimono*, and as he squatted down to perform his daily duty he gave a shrill cry of agony.

Ukifune, having managed to enter the *daimyō*'s residence unobserved, had hidden in the cesspit below the toilet and waited for Kenshin to make his appearance. Thus, Oda Nobunaga's order that the dwarf sleep in an earthenware jar had merely been to prepare the *ninja* for a lengthy wait in cramped conditions.

When the moment was right, Ukifune drove a short

spear up into Kenshin's anus. As the *daimyō*'s screams brought his bodyguards running, Ukifune burrowed out of sight into the accumulated human waste, breathing through a short length of bamboo. Patiently he waited until the dying *daimyō* and his men – who could only assume that the assassin had already got away – had left the lavatory; then emerged to make his escape (and, presumably, to get a bath PDQ).

URQUIDEZ, BENNY 'THE JET'

Urquidez's nickname is due to his highly energetic fighting style and legendary 'jump spinning back kick' that in his heyday put many an opponent flat on their back.

He began his fighting career in 1957 when aged five (although he boasts proudly of having had a pair of boxing gloves by the age of three), competing in the quaintly titled 'Pee wee boxing' events at the Olympic Auditorium in Los Angeles. He came from fighting stock, his mother a wrestler and his father a boxer, both parents competing at a professional level.

Urquidez gained his *karate* black belt aged fourteen (in the 1960s this was something virtually unheard of, and not all too common as it is today). He was therefore obliged to fight much larger and heavier adults, who soon learned to be wary of this teenage upstart.

He began fighting point or 'non-contact' *karate*,

coming to England in 1973 as part of **Ed Parker**'s team: The Los Angeles Stars (who were sponsored by Elvis Presley, himself a *karate* black belt). But Urquidez soon grew dissatisfied with this non-contact style of fighting; he wanted to see whether what he'd learned – and was continuing to learn – would stand up in an 'authentic' environment.

So he entered the World Series of Martial Arts – a gruelling championship with a distinct scarcity of rules and no weight divisions, which he went on to win, in the process establishing full-contact *karate* and what would become known as American kickboxing.

He went to Japan in 1977, winning his first fight against Katsuyuki Suzuki with a knockout in the sixth round. To avenge this, the undefeated fighter Kunimatsu Okau came out of retirement to challenge The Jet, only to be knocked out himself during the fourth round of their fight. The Jet then went on to perform his typical, celebratory back flip.

Since his retirement in 1985, Urquidez has fought only twice, winning both times. He prefers to concentrate on teaching martial arts at his The Jets Gym in California, working as a personal trainer to numerous stars including Tom Cruise and Nicolas Cage, and indulging in his passion for acting. (He has to date made two films with **Jackie Chan** – *Wheels on Meals* and *Dragons Forever*.)

V

VAN DAMME, JEAN-CLAUDE

The 'Muscles from Brussels' (Van Damme has declared that he doesn't mind this nickname, stating that it is at least better than being called 'the idiot from Brussels') was born in 1960, and from childhood studied various martial arts as well as ballet. He competed in his first kickboxing tournament aged sixteen and would spend the next half-decade pursuing an impressive fighting career before deciding to try and make it in films.

(Later, after Van Damme had become famous as an actor – and with some questioning whether he had been as successful in the ring as he claimed [as it transpired he had] – **Don 'The Dragon' Wilson** offered him a $100 000 'bounty fight'. Van Damme declined, however, stating that it was nothing more than a publicity stunt.)

Aged twenty-one, he moved to Los Angeles, speaking only basic English and struggling to support himself with such jobs as pizza deliverer and cab driver.

Changing his last name from Van Varenberg to Van Damme failed to bring him any more acting work (he'd so far scraped by with a couple of bit-parts), and in the end the man who would also become known as the 'King of the Belgians' decided that drastic times called for drastic measures.

So, the very next day, according to legend, a film producer called Menahem Golan was surprised when – leaving a restaurant – a young man suddenly appeared from nowhere to perform a lightning 360-degree kick a mere inch away from his face.

Instead of calling the police, Golan merely requested that Van Damme call by his office the following day, where he presented the young would-be actor with his first proper script.

Bloodsport was a huge success, and was quickly followed by a succession of other action movies – *Double Impact*, *Legionnaire* – that made Van Damme a household name during the late 1980s and '90s. Having confessed to struggling with cocaine addiction in the early 1990s – a problem caused partly by his volatile personal life – Van Damme also revealed that intensive exercise and martial arts' training had been his way of dealing with what was eventually diagnosed as bipolar disorder. This has been effectively treated with sodium valproate – a common medication for this type of mental illness – referred to by Van Damme as 'that simple salt'.

VANDENBERG, DOMINIQUE

Self-described 'pissed-off murderous sociopath', Belgium-born Dominique Vandenberg was enrolled in martial arts' lessons as a child as a 'cure' for his uncontrollable fits of rage.

By the age of eighteen – states the 'blurb' for his autobiography, *The Iron Circle: The True Life Story of Dominique Vandenberg* – he'd become the youngest ever male to win the World Open in Bare Knuckle Karate.

Before this, aged sixteen, he went to the Japanese island of Okinawa to train in the little-known martial art of '*kunto*'.

Military training in Germany came later, and then he began seriously training for a prestigious martial arts' tournament. Disaster struck when he was struck by a speeding car, breaking his leg.

With his dreams of obtaining martial arts' superstardom in tatters, Vandenberg enrolled in the French Foreign Legion, going on to serve in a number of hellholes in Africa.

When he lost his fiancée – a freedom fighter murdered in one such place – Vandenberg abandoned everything and moved to Thailand, where he competed in the bloody freestyle fighting rings (or 'iron circles').

He has since become a respected fight choreographer and actor, appearing in such films as *Mortal Kombat*, *The Doorman,* and *Gangs of New York*.

VIGNY, PIERRE

'Active' (for want of a better word) towards the end of the nineteenth century – but with apparently no record existing of when he was born or died – Pierre Vigny was a specialist in the French stick-fighting discipline known as '*la canne*'. Coming to England, he for a time worked as an instructor at **Edward William Barton-Wright**'s Bartitsu Club. He was skilled in English boxing, the 'health-giving advantages' of which, he declared, 'cannot be too strongly made known' and which thus enabled a man 'to face danger fearlessly'. (Vigny was also more than proficient in wrestling, *savate* and *jujitsu*. Indeed, just like **Barton-Wright,** he was prone to 'testing' his skills by deliberately seeking fights in various places of ill repute, such as gambling dens.)

But Vigny was most taken with the stick or cane; for it was this that corrected any discrepancies – say, for example, in size and weight – that could occur in a 'physical altercation'. Indeed, declared Vigny, if a man knew how to wield a stick correctly, he had no need to fear even 'a bigger and stronger man, though similarly armed'.

In 1903 he opened his own training establishment,

based at 18 Berners Street, London. His classes quickly proved popular, although one man (interestingly described as an 'aristocratic hooligan') who visited – intent on causing Vigny bodily damage and loudly declaring that '... no man has ever been able to stand before me' – ultimately crawled back out with a broken jaw.

Vigny was assisted by his wife who (regardless of her marital status) seems to have been commonly referred to as 'Miss Sanderson'. The good Miss Sanderson was apparently no less lethal than her husband; for in a series of prints entitled *The Defeat of the Hooligan*, she can be seen thrashing a bowler-hatted miscreant with her umbrella. (Miss Sanderson also went on to demonstrate – to her 'target audience' of otherwise genteel Edwardian ladies – how their knees might be used to great effect in depriving a would-be attacker of their front teeth.)

VISITACION, FLORENDO

Popularly known as 'Professor Vee', Florendo Visitacion was born in the Philippine province of Ilocos Norte on 11 June, 1910. He began studying martial arts aged ten, learning an assortment of styles from whoever would consent to teach him. He continued his training after he moved to Hawaii (1926), and from there to America (1928), and during the Second World

War – whilst serving with the US military – relished the opportunity to practise unarmed combat.

He moved to New York at the start of the 1950s, and continued avidly digesting as many different styles of martial arts as he was able; from Chinese *kung-fu* to Mongolian wrestling. Finally, he felt ready to evolve his own style, which he entitled *Vee Jitsu Ryu Jujitsu*. It quickly proved popular, and followed Professor Vee's basic belief that 'maximum effectiveness' should be achieved with 'minimum effort'.

By the time Professor Vee died in January 1999, he had already appointed his successors. As such, *Vee Jitsu Ryu Jujitsu* continues to flourish.

WALLACE, BILL

In his 1970s heyday, Wallace was known as 'Super-foot', kicking at speeds of over sixty miles an hour and stunning audiences (to say nothing of his opponent) with his power and precision.

As a young man (born December 1945), he began his martial arts' training with *judō*, moving onto *karate* while in the United States Air Force. He finally switched to kickboxing, and in the course of his many fights suffered a bad knee injury (which would forever afterwards restrict the use of his right leg) as well as the loss of testicle, in spite of the fact that he was wearing an athletic cup at the time.

Superfoot's fans included Elvis Presley, who in 1973 had the fighter treated at his Graceland Mansion for a non-specified injury.

Wallace retired undefeated as the Professional Karate Association's Middleweight Champion in 1980, and has since worked as a coach, personal trainer, actor, author (with one book entitled, perhaps obviously, *The Ultimate Kick*) television commentator and lecturer.

WHEELER, FLEX

Although he has described himself as being a 'martial artist first, bodybuilder second', 'Flex' Wheeler (born Kenneth Wheeler in 1965) earned the nickname 'The Sultan of Symmetry' due to his truly awesome physique, coming first in the 'Mr California' bodybuilding championships in 1989.

A rare kidney disease led to him undergoing a kidney transplant in 2003, which brought about his retirement from professional bodybuilding. However, he continues to train extensively in martial arts, and particularly in '*kempkwondo*' – a mixture of *kempo* and *tae kwon do*.

WILSON, DON 'THE DRAGON'

The greatest kickboxer of all time? Many would seem to think so. Born in 1954, Wilson started out training in *kung-fu*, but soon made the switch to kickboxing. He turned professional in 1974 and never looked back, becoming the US Middleweight Champion five years later.

He then worked with kickboxing legend Bill 'Superfoot' Wallace, the pair of them perfecting The Dragon's kicks so that he was able to deliver double or even triple kicks with either leg.

Wilson went on to win numerous trophies and tournaments, and in 1983 was named *Official Karate* magazine's 'Fighter of the Year'.

Upon the advice of his friend **Chuck Norris**, Wilson wound down his fighting career to instead concentrate on acting – a gamble that paid off in spectacular fashion when he rocketed to fame in *Bloodfist* (1989).

WONG, FEI HUNG

A Chinese folk hero born in 1847, Wong was trained in martial arts by his father when still a child. So poor were his family that father and son were frequently obliged to travel around the country, performing martial arts' demonstrations and selling traditional medicines.

By the time Wong was in his teens, however, he'd become expert at the Southern Chinese *kung-fu* form known as *Hung Gar*. This emphasised a low, 'horse-saddle'-like stance, and boasted moves with such names as 'Angry Tiger Fist' and 'No Shadow Kick' (something at which Wong is said to have been particularly proficient).

He also became a respected healer, well known for his skill in acupuncture. By all accounts a compassionate man, he attempted to treat all those who came to him for help, regardless of whether or not they had the means with which to pay him.

Wong also joined the Chinese Army to fight against the Japanese in Taiwan, and it is partly because of this that he remains so revered to this day. Factual occurrences taken from his life are freely mixed with fiction, both in print and on the big screen, so that the reader/viewer is led to believe that Wong was able to do such things as fight off thirty assailants armed only with a stick.

Married four times and the father of ten sons (one of whom was shot dead by a drug dealer), Wong Fei Hung died in 1924 at the age of seventy-seven.

WONG, LONG

A young *Shaolin* monk, Wong Long (also often referred to as Wang Lang) was taking a break between martial arts' training one day and, while seated in a wood, happened to observe a fight between a locust and a praying mantis.

It seemed certain that the locust would win, being the larger insect, but every attack it tried to mount was foiled by the mantis, which grabbed hold of and crushed the locust's legs.

Intrigued, Wong Long took the victorious creature back to the temple with him, where he spent some hours prodding it with a stick and observing and cataloguing its movements. He later incorporated these movements into his own martial arts' practise, much to the surprise (and subsequent interest) of the other monks and their teacher. Wong Long had innovated the now-famous 'Praying Mantis' style of *kung-fu*.

WONG, YAN LAM

Wong Yan Lam was another of the *Guangdong Sahp Fu,* or 'Ten Tigers of Canton', along with **Tit Kiu Saam**. Out of all the 'Ten Tigers', Wong Yan Lam was considered the best fighter. He'd previously worked as a bodyguard, and over a three-day period had once been obliged to fight 150 men after bravely declaring that no one could beat his *kung-fu*.

<u>X</u>

XIANGZHAI, WANG

Wang Xiangzhai (1885 *or* 1890–1963) was the founder of *yiquan*, also known as *dachengquan* ('great achievement boxing'). This martial art was (and still is) designed to improve both a person's general health and fighting ability. It placed great emphasis on 'standing meditation' – which Wang claimed activated the 'whole human organism' far better than any other martial art – and rejected a great deal of what Wang disparagingly referred to as 'pretty forms'.

Wang spent much of his life roaming around China, seeking out other martial artists with whom he could exchange ideas (and blows). In fact, in 1939 he took out a full-page advertisement in a Beijing newspaper, asking for those who were expert at fighting to come and see him. History records that of those many men

who did, not one succeeded in beating either Xiangzhai
or any of his four most advanced students, all of whom
had mastered his mysterious 'standing meditation'.

Y

YAGORO

According to legend, aged just fourteen, Yagoro floated across from the Japanese island of Oshima to a little seaside village named Ito on just a piece of wood.

In Ito Yagoro initially earned a less-than-enthusiastic reception, due to the distrust that the inhabitants of such villages traditionally held for 'outsiders'. However, this dramatically changed when six bandits sought to attack the village, only to be single-handedly dispatched by the teenager who wielded nothing more than a wooden stick.

In reward, the villagers clubbed together to supply Yagoro with the money he needed to seek out a *sensei* ('teacher') who could fulfil his earnest desire to become a master swordsman. They also gave him a proper *katana* (sword).

From Ito Yagoro travelled to a famous shrine, where for six days and nights he meditated and practised his technique with his new sword.

On the seventh night, however, he was surprised from behind by an unknown attacker, who sought to assassinate the young man. Somehow sensing the attack – and moving as quick as lightning – Yagoro turned, drew his sword, and struck down his would-be assassin in one fluid movement.

He had, unwittingly, just perfected his 'signature' technique; the very heart of the style that he would go on to label *Itto Ryu* – 'One Sword'.

YAMAGUCHI, GOGEN

Born in Japan in 1909, Yamaguchi would famously become known as 'The Cat' due to his long hair and fast and distinctly feline way of moving. Obsessed with *karate* from a young age, he was expelled from Kansai University for fighting. Undaunted, Yamaguchi moved to another university, where he established a *karate* club that was soon renowned for the iron-hard training it offered. (Indeed, many students attested that there was little difference between the '*karate*' offered by Yamaguchi and plain old street fighting.)

Fiercely patriotic, Yamaguchi (who stood little more

than five feet tall) had a shadowy role in Manchuria during the Second World War. He is variously described as having been an 'intelligence officer', a 'spy', or some kind of 'undercover agent', and on one occasion disarmed a man who'd been about to shoot him with series of lightning kicks.

Later captured by the Russians, Yamaguchi spent two years in a Mongolian slave-labour camp, somehow surviving appalling conditions (and, according to his autobiography, on one occasion killing a tiger with his bare hands) to return to Tokyo in 1947.

Yamaguchi was devastated by the damage his beloved country suffered during the war. Further considering that Japan's defeat had caused the country irreparable spiritual decline, Yamaguchi felt so distressed that he decided to commit suicide by *seppuku* – the ancient *samurai* practise of self-disembowelment. As he was about to do this, however, he experienced what he later described as a 'divine revelation'. It was not his duty to kill himself, he realised, but to instead teach martial arts and assist Japan in its recovery following the war.

He went on to integrate yoga breathing practises into his training, and espoused what is today commonly known as the 'mind–body connection'. Having founded the International Karate-do Goju Kai Association, and having done much to spread the practise of *karate* around the world, Yamaguchi was awarded the

'Blue Ribbon Medal' by Emperor Hirohito in 1968. He'd achieved the ultimate *karate* ranking of tenth *dan* by the time he passed away in 1989.

YANG, LU-CH'AN

Pioneering teacher of *tai chi chuan* ('the supreme ultimate fist'). In 1850, at the age of fifty, Yang Lu-ch'an was poached from the martial arts' school he'd helped to found by the Chinese Emperor himself, who desired Yang to teach what he knew to the royal bodyguard. It was this, as much as anything else, that established *tai chi*'s massive popularity within China.

Yang Lu-ch'an possessed several nicknames pertaining to his general physical hardness, such as 'Yang the Invincible' and 'Yang the Unsurpassed'. It was rumoured that when he first went to meet the Emperor, he was attacked by a couple of guard dogs. The unfortunate creatures, however, lost their teeth when they made the mistake of biting Yang's iron-hard legs.

On another occasion, a man sought to prove that Yang wasn't really so tough after all by punching the martial arts' master as hard as he could in the stomach. Yang apparently did nothing more than laugh – the force of his breath sending his aggressor sprawling.

YARA, CHATAN

A *karate* master from the Japanese island of Okinawa, born around 1670, who from the age of twelve was sent to live and work in China for a period of twenty years. He returned fluent in Chinese, and was thus able to secure himself employment as a translator.

Chatan Yara was fond of taking early morning walks along the beach, to meditate and think through the forthcoming day's work. One morning, while doing just this, he heard the stifled screams of a young woman.

Yara quickly found her, a Japanese *samurai* on top of her, the pair almost concealed by the thick vegetation that bordered the beach.

'Please, help me!' pleaded the woman as she saw Yara, stark terror in her eyes. 'This man is going to rape me!'

Yara bit back on his fear. 'Let the woman go,' he told the *samurai* tonelessly.

The *samurai* briefly paused in what he was doing to look at the young man.

'Leave now, boy, and I'll let you live,' he growled, before returning his attention to the woman.

Yara took notice of the *samurai*'s sword, and realised that he needed a weapon of his own. But there was nothing.

'Let her go,' he repeated, certain that within a few moments he'd be dead. An air of calm fatalism filled his mind: if he had to die to prevent a woman from being raped, so be it.

'I warned you,' said the *samurai* tiredly, as though this really was a distraction he could do without. He picked himself up off the woman, and advanced with his sword drawn towards Yara.

More for amusement than with any real deadly intent, the *samurai* swiped at Yara once, twice, with his sword. In any moment Yara's head would be lying on the sand, thought the *samurai* – did it matter if he briefly toyed with the *Okinawan*?

'Go on, get out of here!' Yara told the woman, who got to her feet and ran over to where a small rowboat was lying on the sand. Grabbing an old oar from inside the boat, she threw it over to Yara.

'Here – use this!' she told him.

Yara was expert in the use of the *bÿ* – a staff made from hard wood. So using the paddle end of the oar, he brought it crashing down on the *samurai*'s head, killing the man instantly.

Retribution for this 'crime' would surely come from other Japanese *samurai* and soldiers, and so the woman Yara had saved took him to her village that was up in the mountains. There Yara lived quietly for many years, sheltered by – and teaching his martial arts to – the villagers.

YEN, DONNIE

Yen was born in Canton, China, on 27 July, 1963, but moved to Boston, USA, at the age of eleven. His mother – noted martial arts' expert Bow Sim-Mark – instructed him in *tai chi chuan* from the age of four, although as he grew older Yen experimented with a number of other martial arts, including *tae kwon do* and *wushu*.

It was *wushu* that Yen decided to pursue, something that prompted his move to Beijing where he joined the Beijing Wushu Team. (Apparently, his instructor there soon demanded that Yen lose his Western-influenced, mullet-style haircut, deeming it less than appropriate.)

A trip to Hong Kong resulted in Yen meeting Yuen Woo-Ping, the well-known film director, who was instrumental in securing Yen's first film role (aged twenty-one) in the movie *Xiao Tai Ji*.

Although *Xiao Tai Ji* was not a great success, it at least allowed Yen to begin his film career – which would pay off in spectacular fashion with *Once Upon a Time in China II* (1992), best known for Yen's character General Lan's final, epic fight against **Jet Li's** Wong Fei Hung.

YUAN-PIN, CHEN

During the Ming Dynasty, a general named Chen Yuan-Pin was obliged to beat a hasty retreat from

China when a price was put upon his head by the authorities. (For what reason does not appear to have been recorded.)

Despite his military ranking, he was at first regarded as being a bit of a softie by those Japanese who met him; he was a quiet, slightly-built man, with a love of poetry and calligraphy. Indeed, so genteel did he appear that he was frequently mocked by the *samurai* who inhabited the area (today part of Tokyo).

Yuan-Pin was soon recruited into the service of a shogun, who requested that the Chinese general teach art and literature within his castle. Yuan-Pin refused to live within the castle grounds, however, preferring each evening to return to a temple where he'd obtained lodgings.

Concerned for Yuan-Pin's safety, the shogun ordered three of his *samurai* warriors to accompany him home, as the nights were dark and the area outside of the castle infested with bandits. One evening, as the four men walked through a deserted wood, they were attacked by a group of cut-throats.

The *samurai* fought valiantly, but were hopelessly outnumbered. Just when all seemed lost, however, Yuan-Pin leapt into action, moving faster than the wind and dispatching all of the attackers with a series of lightning moves.

From then on, their opinion of the Chinaman some-what altered by what they'd witnessed, the three *samu-*

rai begged Yuan-Pin to teach him what he knew. Finally, Yuan-Pin agreed, and the *samurai* became expert in *wushu,* and they in turn took on students themselves.

However, oft-repeated claims that this proves that all Japanese martial arts have their roots in China are, said **Donald F. Draeger**, about 'as valid as implying that the inventor of the wheel was the developer of the modern automobile'.

YUE, FEI

A military general who lived during China's Song Dynasty (which was, incidentally, the first government in China – and quite possibly the world – to issue paper money), Yue Fei's second name means 'fly'.

This was in reference to the fact that a supernatural bird called a *Peng* (which also had the ability to transform itself into a fabulous fish) alighted on the roof of Yue's parents' house at the time of his birth – something that was considered to be rather a good omen.

Certainly, Yue Fei grew up to be a healthy and virile young man, possessed of near-superhuman strength and expert with both a bow and a spear. His mother had had the words 'Be Loyal to Motherland' (*sic*) tattooed on his back at an early age, and this was to be Yue's motto throughout his life. (To this day, Yue is considered a hero by many Chinese people for his discipline and bravery.)

As well as with weapons, Yue was also expert at unarmed martial arts, paying particular attention to *qigong* – the use of the body's own energy field, and the art of correct breathing to enhance one's health and physical endeavour.

Either a Buddhist hermit or the monks of the *Shaolin* Temple (or perhaps both) taught him 'iron shirt', where the body is conditioned to withstand any blow. He is also said to have mastered any number of different *Shaolin* boxing and wrestling techniques.

Reports vary on how he met his death in 1142, aged just thirty-eight, although one explanation details how a false charge of treason led to him being imprisoned and tortured.

Refusing to admit to his 'guilt', Yue Fei was surprised by two burly prison guards one night and strangled to death with a thick rope.

YUEN, WOO PING

Pioneering Chinese martial arts' choreographer and film director (born 1945), Yuen Woo Ping has for many years been one of the most influential figures in Hong Kong action cinema, where 'Hollywood-like' action meets traditional Eastern storylines and settings. There are, however, a range of film styles; from earthy *kung-fu* movies right through to more mystical, 'swords and sorcery'-type features.

In his youth Yuen Woo Ping was a member of the Peking Opera School (for more information concerning the Peking Opera School, refer also to entries for **Jackie Chan** and **Sammo Hung**), and came to prominence when he directed Chan's groundbreaking 1978 movie *Drunken Master*. His fame grew within the industry over the following years, peaking with his work as an action choreographer on the masterful *Crouching Tiger, Hidden Dragon* (2000).

YUKSA, KUMGANG

At the entrance of Sokkul Am, a Buddhist cave temple in Korea, there is a stone carving of the famous warrior-monk Kumgang Yuksa. He served during the reign of King Hye Gong (742–762 AD), and the fact that he is depicted in a typical martial arts' posture is used by many martial arts' historians as 'proof' that the fighting arts existed in Korea from ancient times, and were not (as is so often claimed) imported via China or India.

The fighting art Kumgang Yuksa would have learned was known as *taek kyon* ('foot fighting') – the predecessor to *tae kwon do* – which from the fifth or sixth century onwards was practised by the ruling elite as well as their protectors.

By the fifteenth century, however, *taek kyon*'s popularity had become so widespread that even the lowliest peasant working in the paddy fields could be found indulging in an hour's practise every day.

This struck something of a death-knell for *taek kyon*, as it was hurriedly abandoned by the 'higher' classes in favour of more genteel pursuits, such as poetry and drawing.

Soon Korea's premier fighting system was considered by many to be nothing more than a crude and outdated pastime – something that was fit to be practised only by the roughest of individuals.